The Midnight Hour

Bright Ideas for After Dark

BY GEOFF EDGERS

SCHOLASTIC INC.

New York   Toronto   London
Auckland   Sydney

Written by sleepaholic **Geoff Edgers**
Cover design by **C. Shane** "Snoozy" **Sykes**
Interior design by narcoleptic **MKR Design, Inc.**
(which is ruled by her slumbering highness **Marta Ruliffson**)
Illustrations by the sleep-deprived **Joe Bartos**, nap-happy **Tim
Haggerty** and "I'm just naturally peppy" **Matt Straub**
Cover illustration by **Jack** "drowsy guy" **Keely**

ISBN 0-590-68291-1

Copyright © 1997 by The Editors of Planet Dexter.
Illustrations copyright © 1997 by Joe Bartos, Tim Haggerty, and Matt Straub.
All rights reserved. Published by Scholastic Inc., 555 Broadway, New York, NY 10012,
by arrangement with Addison Wesley Longman.

The Midnight Hour

BRIGHT IDEAS FOR AFTER DARK

The Plan

It's Dark Out.
YOU'RE ALONE.
Here's What
To Do.

So you're in bed. You've pulled up the sheets, pulled down the shades and said "Good night!" to anyone within earshot.

Time to hit the hay, right?

Nah!

In case you didn't know, we each spend one-third of our lives in bed. That means eight hours a day, 56 hours a week, 224 hours a month, 2,688 hours a year, 26,880 hours a . . . all right, you get the picture. Wouldn't it be silly to waste all that time catching ZZZZZs?

Of course, some folks will tell you bedtime is for shut-eye and shut-eye alone. These folks might even be your parents. Don't blame them, they're just doing their job. They probably heard the same thing when they were kids. Not that it kept them from hiding books and tiny transistor radios under the covers.

Bed is your secret place. Think about anything — even chocolate cake for breakfast. Curl yourself into a ball and sing the National Anthem in Swedish. Nobody's going to stop you. (Just don't try this in a movie theater!)

With a little imagination, bed can become your private reading room. That's where the flashlight comes in.

Put this book on your pillow, lie on your belly, and pull the covers up so they fall over your arms and shoulders but not your head. (It can get hot under there.) Wait until the adults are somewhere else. Flick on your flashlight. There. Now you're ready.

Sleep Tidbits
How MUCH Do You REALLY Need?

Babies get 16 hours a day. Most adults shoot for 8. Valentine Medina, a 75-year-old man from Spain, told the *Guinness Book of World Records* he stopped sleeping in 1904. He didn't sleep for about 70 years! And you? Good question.

You see, everyone has his or her own requirements for sleep. It depends on how you feel. As a general rule, 10-year-old kids are supposed to get 10 hours. Here's a hint: if you feel tired or slow or sleepy or sluggish during the day, you need more. If you get only 9 hours and feel like a million bucks, maybe you don't.

Here's a quick survey to help you figure out whether you're getting enough sleep:

1 When you walk down the street, do you start snoring?

2 Have you ever suspected your bus driver of being the Tooth Fairy?

3 Do you have many nightmares when you're doing your math homework?

(If you answered yes to at least two of three questions, you might have a problem.)

Sleep is important. In Oklahoma and California, 20 percent of highway accidents in one year involved sleepy drivers. In 1959, a man named Peter Tripp didn't sleep for 200 hours. What happened? He started hallucinating — seeing things! A suit made of worms. Flames coming out of a drawer. Who needs that?

Sleep also helps you get better when you're sick. During sleep, the body mobilizes the cells that form our natural defense against illness. Also, it is during sleep that we produce more of something called the human growth hormone, which, as you might suspect, helps us grow.

So there's the choice: car crashes and hallucinations on one side, cell production and growth on the other. You make the call.

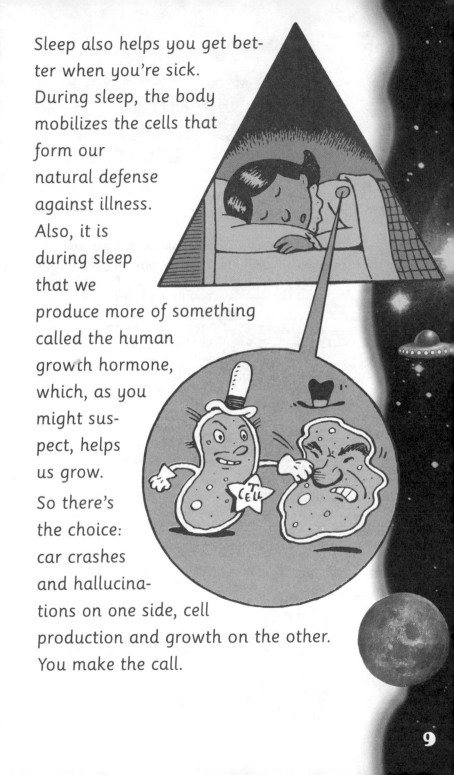

5 FAMOUS SHORT SLEEPERS

1 Napoleon Bonaparte, conqueror

Napoleon would wake up at three o'clock in the morning and demand his secretary be ready with pen and paper to take down his every thought until it got light outside. If you're considering doing the same with a younger sister or brother, remember one thing: Napoleon died in exile.

2 Thomas Edison, inventor

Edison once slept 36 straight hours, but only after staying up several days in a row. It seems he had the phonograph to invent and the light bulb to perfect. (Good excuse.) "Sleep is an acquired habit," Edison once said. "Cells don't sleep. Fish swim in the water all night. Even a horse doesn't sleep. Man doesn't need to sleep." When would he see the light?

3 Margaret Thatcher, former British Prime Minister

Thatcher had a reputation for putting in 18-hour days. This meant waking up with the sun, returning home past 11 P.M. and, after a quick supper, taking care of paperwork until 1 or 2 A.M.

No sleep makes Maggie a dull minister.

4 Isaac Asimov, science-fiction writer

"I never use an alarm clock," he said. "In the army I always woke up before reveille. I hate sleeping. It wastes time." Maybe he really was from outer space!

5 David Brenner, comedian

When he was eight years old, Brenner determined that by sleeping just 4 hours a night — instead of 8 — he could save about 1,456 hours a year. If he lives to be 80, Brenner will have saved 104,832 hours. A little math goes a long way.

JET LAG

When you travel to another time zone, your sleep schedule gets all messed up. Take a trip from New York to Los Angeles, for example. There's a three-hour time difference, so if you arrive in LA at 8 P.M., your body is telling you it's really 11 P.M. (the time in New York).

Hollywood Tips
A Little Hint that Could Make You a Big Success

So you want to make a movie. Who doesn't? Fortunately, this page contains a vital piece of information no young filmmaker should traverse Tinseltown without. It has nothing to do with big budgets or signing up Tom Cruise. The secret to getting a movie made may be more basic: put "**Night**" in your movie title.

Look how many times it has worked before:

Night Nurse (1931); **Night** World (1932); **Night** after **Night** (1932); **Night** Court (1932); **Night** of Terror (1933); **Night** at the Opera (1935); **Night** Club Scandal (1937); **Night** Must Fall (1937); **Night** of Mystery (1937); **Night** Key (1937); The **Night** of January 16th (1941); The **Night** has Eyes (1942); **Night** Monster (1942); A **Night** in New Orleans (1942); **Night**mare (1942); A **Night** to Remember (1943); **Night** Plane from Chungking (1943); A **Night** in Paradise (1946); **Night** and Day (1946); A **Night** in Casablanca (1946); **Night**mare Alley (1947); **Night** Song (1947); **Night** Has a Thousand Eyes (1948); **Night** Unto **Night** (1947); **Night** and the City (1950); **Night** into Morning (1951); **Night** Without Sleep (1952); **Night** People (1954); **Night** Freight (1955); The **Night** Holds Terror (1955); The **Night** of the Hunter (1955); **Night**fall (1956); **Night**mare (1956); **Night** Passage (1957); The **Night** Runner (1957);

The **Night** the World Exploded (1957); The **Night** Heaven Fell (1958); **Night** of the Blood Beast (1958); **Night**fighters (1960); **Night** Tide (1963); **Night**mare in the Sun (1964); The **Night** of the Iguana (1964); The **Night** Walker (1964); **Night** Caller from Outer Space (1965); The **Night** of the Grizzly (1966); **Night** of the Living Dead (1968); The **Night** They Raided Minsky's (1968); **Night** Gallery (1969);

Nightmare in Wax (1969); The **Night** of the Following Day (1969); **Night** Chase (1970); **Night** Slaves (1970); The **Night** Visitor (1970); The **Night** Stalker (1971); **Night** of Dark Shadows (1971); The **Night** Digger (1971); The **Night** Evelyn Came Out of the Grave (1971); The **Night**comers (1972); The **Night** Stranger (1972); **Night** of the Lepus (1972); **Night** Flight from Moscow (1973); **Night**mare Honeymoon (1973); **Night** Moves (1975); **Night**mare in Blood (1976); **Night** Creature (1978); A **Night** Full of Rain (1978); **Night**wing (1979); **Night** Games (1980); **Night** of the Juggler (1980); **Night** Crossing

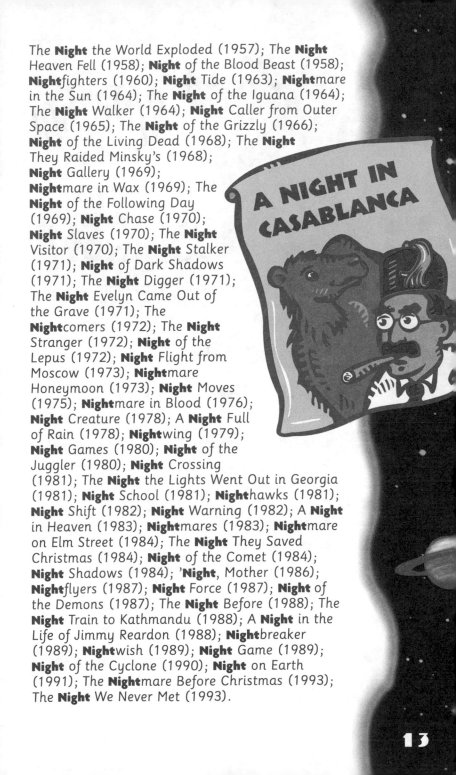

A NIGHT IN CASABLANCA

(1981); The **Night** the Lights Went Out in Georgia (1981); **Night** School (1981); **Night**hawks (1981); **Night** Shift (1982); **Night** Warning (1982); A **Night** in Heaven (1983); **Night**mares (1983); **Night**mare on Elm Street (1984); The **Night** They Saved Christmas (1984); **Night** of the Comet (1984); **Night** Shadows (1984); 'Night, Mother (1986); **Night**flyers (1987); **Night** Force (1987); **Night** of the Demons (1987); The **Night** Before (1988); The **Night** Train to Kathmandu (1988); A **Night** in the Life of Jimmy Reardon (1988); **Night**breaker (1989); **Night**wish (1989); **Night** Game (1989); **Night** of the Cyclone (1990); **Night** on Earth (1991); The **Night**mare Before Christmas (1993); The **Night** We Never Met (1993).

The Slumber Screen

DID YOU KNOW

that former President Ronald Reagan starred in the 1951 movie "Bedtime for Bonzo"? The Prez plays a professor who treats his chimp like his kid for an experiment.

What a novel idea!

MATCH THE MOVIE

WITH THE STAR

1. "Bedtime for Bonzo"
2. "Bedtime Story"
3. "Dreamboat"
4. "Dream Lover"
5. "Night at the Opera"
6. "Night and the City"
7. "Nightmare on Elm Street"
8. "Night Shift"
9. "The Night We Never Met"

a. Kristy McNichol
b. Jessica Lange
c. Ronald Reagan
d. Johnny Depp
e. Marlon Brando
f. Ginger Rogers
g. The Marx Brothers
h. Matthew Broderick
i. Michael Keaton

Answers: 1. c; 2. e; 3. f; 4. a; 5. g; 6. b; 7. d; 8. i; 9. h.

DREAM ON

Can you guess which TV show or movie contains the following scenarios?

1. This big dream takes a young girl from home. To get back, all she has to do is click your heels, say "There's no place like home," and open her eyes.

a. "Dallas"

2. Bobby gets hit by a car and dies. So do the ratings of this popular TV program. Surprise, surprise! Bobby returns. It was all just his wife's dream.

b. "Nightmare on Elm Street"

3. If you fall asleep, Freddy Kreuger can get you in your dreams. And you will never come back. Don't worry — it's just a movie.

c. "The Simpsons."

4. Homer, in a dream, gets permission from God to skip Church — much to Marge's objections.

d. "The Wizard of Oz."

Answers: 1. d; 2. a; 3. b; 4 c.

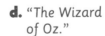

NIGHT LIFE
In 1843, the world's first night club opened in Paris. It was called *Le Cal des Anglais.*

15

WHILE YOU WERE SLEEPING . . . Weird Stuff WAS HAPPENING

When you close your eyes and drift off, you might think you're just sleeping. But your body is still on duty. "Take a vacation," you want to tell it. But it is not interested in a trip to Disney World, or even a day at the beach. See, your body has to have structure and order, even when you're drifting off.

The body divides each night into five stages.

First, we begin to nod off. Slowly. If you've ever felt your body jerk itself awake, suddenly, when you're almost asleep, fear not. That's called a <u>hypnagogic jerk</u>. It's totally harmless, except for one thing: it can throw us back to square one — being awake.

In Stage One, you might see people and hear sounds that aren't there. Your brain is confused. It doesn't know whether it's working for someone who is asleep or awake. So if you're positive Abraham Lincoln visited your bedroom last night to check out your pogs, think again. You are probably in Stage One.

xytriz lomick

Stage Two is a 25- to 50-minute period is when most people talk in their sleep. The talk is almost always meaningless babble. This is sometimes very entertaining. Your body gets about two degrees colder; your heart pumps less. Ever put your hand over your heart after running? The thumping is the blood being pumped fast to gives you more oxygen. When you sleep, you don't need as much. Hence, the slow pump.

Stage Three: your muscles go limp and you get very confused if somebody wakes you up.

Stage Four: you're so asleep you might toss aside the covers, stand up and start walking around without knowing it. Nightmares love Stage Four, probably because they know Stage Five is coming.

Stage Five is when we dream. More on that later.

GETTING SLEEPY?
Turn out the flashlight if you want. There's always tomorrow.

To Nap OR NOT TO NAP ?

◆

Painter Salvador Dali loved to nap. But only for a minute. He would hold a spoon in his hand. When he fell asleep, the spoon would fall to the ground and wake him up. "Good enough," he'd shrug and go on his way.

Eleanor Roosevelt often took one-minute naps in public, even during White House dinners.

zzzzzzzzzz

THE FISH EYE

Fish sleep with their eyes open for one good reason: they have no eyelids. A fish blocks out light the same way our ears block out sound during our sleep.

TOO TRUE

"The amount of sleep required by the average person is about five minutes more."
— Max Kauffman.

Other famous nappers include Napoleon, John F. Kennedy, Thomas Edison, and Barbara Walters.

It's hard to say whether napping helps you sleep better. Try it. If it helps, keep napping. If it doesn't, go fishing, or save the whales.

And if anyone asks you how you get anything done if you're always catching a few **Z-Z-Z-Z-Zs,** just tell 'em you're sleeping on it.

19

TOOTH TALK

You're **supposed** to brush your teeth after breakfast, lunch, and dinner, and when you wake up and go to bed. So here's a question: if you're doing everything right, how many times will you end up brushing a day; a week; a year?

We'll help you. It's 5 times a day, 35 times a week, 1,820 times a year. Is it any wonder Americans go through one billion tubes of toothpaste a year?

QUESTION: With all that brushing, why do 90 percent of us have cavities?

ANSWER: It all comes down to how much you brush and what foods you eat.

How come all the good stuff is so bad?

On a scale of worst to best, the worst foods are sticky, gooey, sugary treats like candy bars, and the best are fresh fruits and vegetables. The key is to eat foods that don't stick to your teeth so long they might as well take out a mortgage on your

molars. Ideally, food should shout a quick hello as it heads down your throat.

As a rule, if you want to eat something besides cauliflower for dessert — and you do — show some consideration for your teeth. For example, when you crave candy, grab a Three Musketeers bar, not a Milky Way. The nougat on the Three Musketeers comes off your teeth a little easier than the sticky ingredients in a Milky Way. Gummy Bears are bad news; same for fruit roll-ups.

Raisins are also a poor choice. As you chew, bits of raisin stuff themselves into the cracks and crevices of your mouth. And like many dried fruits, raisins contain extra sugar. Sugar loves eating away at shiny, white teeth. Don't let it.

For snack purposes, choose peanuts instead of raisins. Popcorn is even better than that — as long as you remember to floss for lingering kernels after eating.

The best advice: keep brushing. We hope your teeth will be shiny and white. If not, there's always Dentifrice, a paste invented in France that makes your gums pinker so your teeth look whiter in comparison.

Now for a Little
Tooth Quiz

1. Toothpicks in Ancient Mesopotamia were made of:
   a. wood
   b. beef jerky
   c. gold

2. Before the invention of the toothbrush, teeth were cleaned with:
   a. vacuum cleaners
   b. thin roots connected to wood
   c. your index finger

3. An ancient remedy for a toothache was to:
   a. eat a mouse
   b. dance the Charleston
   c. chew grape gum

4. The first modern toothbrush was invented in:
   a. 1938 b. 1428 c. 1838

5. One substance people did not brush their teeth with was:
   a. charcoal
   b. chalk
   c. a dead monkey's eyeball

Answers: 1. c; 2. b; 3. a; 4. a; 5. c.

Uh-oh
About 47 percent of Americans have never been to the dentist.

GHOST HUNTER

ELLIOT O'DONNELL:

For 60 years, Elliot O'Donnell hunted ghosts all around the world. His journals, published in 1971, recorded encounters with haunted trees, well-meaning werewolves, and the requisite tortured ghoul whose soul will never rest.

O'Donnell had a quality that made his job as ghost-recorder easy: he trusted virtually everyone.

Here are three stories told to him and recorded in his journals:

The Strangling Ghost

An informant told O'Donnell about a haunted double bed in Brugges, Belgium. In that bed, anyone sleeping on the left side faced a night of throttling. (On the right side, you were fine.)

Two businessmen, staying together in the room, learned this first-hand. The man on the right side of the bed woke up in the middle of the night to see his companion struggling to breathe. Looking in the mirror, the man saw a shadowy figure in a black hood learning over his colleague and clutching the man's throat.

After hesitating for a moment, the man on the right side of the bed jumped up and turned on the light in the room. The figure disappeared and the man who had been under attack regained his composure. He talked of bony fingers on his neck, and of feeling the life being squeezed out of him.

The Haunted Shrubs

A psychiatrist told O'Donnell about a former patient named George Gill, who told the doctor about an incident that occurred when he was walking down a road on a rainy night.

A tall, slender woman approached and asked Gill if she could walk with him. When she learned he had a long way to go, the woman invited him into her house for a warm drink. As Gill walked up the front path, he heard a giggle. He turned and there was nothing, just the shrubs. Later, while leaving, he heard it again. The woman told him her name was Ysolde Hairens and invited Gill back the following Thursday.

A few days passed and somehow Gill mixed up his days. He returned one day early — Wednesday — and made his way up the path. Sure enough, as he arrived at the house, he heard the giggling. The door was slightly ajar, so Gill pushed it open.

There, with her back facing away from him, sat Ysolde in front of a mirror. From behind, she looked like the woman he had met the other night. But the reflection in the mirror revealed a face with yellow skin covered in long pimples, a hole where a nose should be, and a slit for a mouth with tusks like a pig.

Spotting Gill, the beast attacked, knocking him to the ground unconscious. When he woke up, the beast was gone, as was the house. A bare, abandoned building remained in its place.

The Phantom of Mannheim Forest

A Pennsylvanian businessman was riding his horse back from a meeting when, as he neared a great forest, a storm began. He pushed on, through thunder and lightning, until the rain stopped and he could continue under the bright moonlight.

Suddenly, a harsh scream sounded through the woods. The man's horse stopped short, throwing him to the ground. Lying there, stunned from the fall, he saw a tall, dark figure with long, messy hair scamper by.

The next day, the man told his story to a friend and learned that everyone who lived in the area stayed away from the forest at night. Turned out the place was known for this screaming creature. As the story went, a woman had been placed in a local psychiatric hospital 20 years earlier. The doctors were told by her husband she needed discipline, so they beat and tortured her. One day, not long after she'd been committed, the woman was found dead in the woods. Her throat had been cut.

The hospital called it a suicide, but nobody could explain how she'd escaped from her cell. And that's when the screams began: first in the hospital, later in the woods.

Questions

Questions

Why does milk sour?

One word: bacteria. Milk is an excellent place for most bacteria to live and build a large family — sort of like the suburbs. The only way you can really prevent bacterial growth is by boiling the milk, which kills all the little guys. But before you consider drinking a piping hot glass, consider that even if you don't like the way sour milk tastes, it's not at all dangerous to drink. In fact, countless recipes require sour milk. And what do you think yogurt is made of?

Why doesn't it hurt when we cut our hair and nails?

Our hair and our finger- and toe-nails are the only parts of our body that don't have nerves. Hence, you could run over them with a Monster truck and you wouldn't feel a thing. (This is not recommended.) Our hair and nails are also the only parts of the body that continue to grow after almost everything else stops growing in our late teens. (One important myth to dispel: hair and nails don't grow after death. They only appear to because the flesh around them shrinks. Yuck!)

How far can we see?

The higher above sea level we are, the farther we can see. This is because the earth is round and the land and sea curve down and away from us. If you are standing at a spot one mile high, with no obstructions, you should be able to see about 96 miles ahead.

Why are tears salty?

The fluids in the human body are naturally salty. Some people say this is because humans evolved from creatures that lived in the sea. Whatever the reason, if you get fresh water in your eye, you'll notice it doesn't mix.

What is colder, wood or marble?

The materials themselves are the same temperature. But it doesn't take a rocket scientist to conclude that marble always feels colder. And even though the steel head of a hammer and a wooden handle are also the same temperature, the steel always feels colder.

The reason has to do with how an object takes our own body heat away from us. Marble and steel are good conductors of heat. Wood is not. Because it doesn't take much heat from our hands, we think it is not so cold.

Do we see a thing instantly when we look at it?

No, and we also don't stop seeing it as soon as we stop looking at it. Sight, like hearing and other sensations, takes as long as it takes for the sensory device — in this case the retina — to communicate the image to the brain. Since it only takes a few hundredths of a second for the brain to receive an image that has reached the back of the eye, we don't notice any delay.

Why do the eyes in some paintings follow you?

Have you ever noticed the paintings in an art gallery staring at you? Don't be freaked out. The eyes in some photos and paintings seem to be able to connect with the eyes of the observer, no matter where he's standing. This is the result of the model's pose. If the model looked directly at the artist when being painted, the subject will look right at you, the viewer, no matter where you stand. How rude!

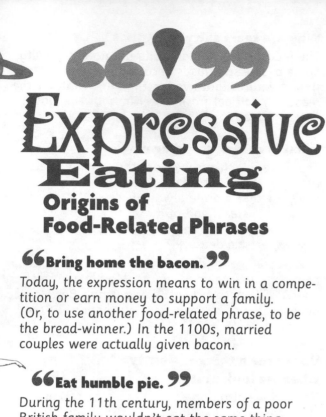

"!" Expressive Eating

Origins of Food-Related Phrases

"Bring home the bacon."

Today, the expression means to win in a competition or earn money to support a family. (Or, to use another food-related phrase, to be the bread-winner.) In the 1100s, married couples were actually given bacon.

"Eat humble pie."

During the 11th century, members of a poor British family wouldn't eat the same thing. The best meat went to the hunter who captured dinner and his favorite sons and friends. The "umbles" — the heart, liver, tongue, brain, kidneys, and entrails — went to his wife and daughters. To make these less-than-desirable mystery meats easier to swallow, the "umbles" would be baked in a pie.

66 Take the cake. 99

Years ago, in contests held in the south, the person with the most imaginative strut — called a cakewalk — would actually receive a cake for the first prize.

66 Make a toast. 99

When the Greeks started this tradition in the 6th century B.C., it had nothing to do with wishing someone good luck. They wanted to demonstrate to guests that the wine hadn't been poisoned.

66 Eat one's hat. 99

"Hatte" was once a European concoction made of eggs, veal, salt, tongue, kidney, and fat. It was not for a weak stomach, so often people would offer to eat "hatte" if they lost a bet.

66 Give the cold shoulder. 99

This is what we're doing when we ignore or snub someone. But in the Middle Ages, any guest who stayed too long received a platter of cold beef shoulder.

Memo-rize this Stuff

(YOU'LL KNOW MORE ABOUT SPACE)

Our Solar System Has Nine Planets:

1 Earth (our personal favorite)

2 Jupiter (the biggest planet)

3 Mars (is there life here?)

4 Mercury (orbits the sun in only 88 days)

5 Neptune (windier than Chicago)

6 Pluto (tiny and coated with methane ice)

7 Saturn (think rings)

8 Uranus (has the longest seasons)

9 Venus (shielded by acid clouds)

These terms come in handy when you're talking space:

Asteroids Minor planets and rocky debris that orbit the sun. Many are found between Jupiter and Mars.

Black Hole An area with a strong gravitational pull that usually surrounds a collapsed star. Light is literally sucked into it, unable to escape, because of the pressure.

Comet An object made of ice and various gases. It begins to dissolve as it nears the sun, producing a tail that can stretch over 100 million kilometers.

Constellation A section, or snapshot, of the sky used to organize objects in space.

Galaxy Gigantic parts of the universe, containing as much as 100 billion to one trillion stars. Galaxies are made up of stars, dust, asteroids, and gas (called nebulae).

Light-Year The distance a beam of light will travel in one year: 5.88 trillion miles.

Lunar Eclipse When the moon passes through the shadow thrown by Earth.

Meteor An asteroid or other space object that heats up and burns when it reaches our atmosphere, creating the falling star effect.

Meteorite Larger than a meteor. Can create a huge crater when it smashes into Earth.

Milky Way The name we've given to our own galaxy.

Orbit The path a planet, star, or any other object takes.

Dexteroid This really doesn't mean anything, but it sounds cool.

Satellite A body that orbits another. The moon, for example, is a satellite of Earth.

Shooting Star What we call a meteor burning away in the atmosphere.

Solar Eclipse When the moon passes between the sun and Earth, blocking the sun from our view.

Star Gas that shines because of an internal nuclear reaction.

Supernova A violent explosion, due to the total destruction of an old, collapsed star or collapse of a massive super-giant star.

White Dwarf An old, collapsed star that has used up all of its energy.

Zodiac The 12 constellations around the orbit of Earth.

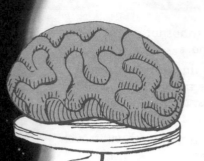

Did You

- **Babies have more bones than adults** — 350 to 200 — because as we get older, many of our bones join up, fusing together. There are 656 muscles in the human body.

- **The average human brain** weighs three pounds and contains 14,000,000,000 cells.

- **There are 72 letters** in the Cambodian alphabet. Rotokas, a language spoken in the South Pacific, has only 11. German, Dutch and English have the same number: 26.

- **Most of us need 2,000 words** to communicate. But the 50 most common words in English account for half of what the average person says and writes. **The words "I" and "you" take up 10 percent of every conversation.**

- **Five thousand languages** have been identified on Earth.

Know...

- **Why do we get lumps** in our throats? Think of your throat as a tunnel lined with muscle. When you swallow, the muscles create a downward, wave-like ripple that makes it easy to get food into your stomach. When we want to cry, the throat muscles tighten. The motion is reversed — from downward to upward. It feels like a lump or knot, and becomes hard to swallow.

- **Humans smell** up to 10,000 different odors.

- **Green potato chips** are merely sunburned. They emerged from underground and refused to use sunblock.

- **Mosquitoes rest on your skin** before biting. When they finally decide to chow, it takes about a minute to cut into the skin and insert the all-important blood-sucking lancet. **Mosquitoes suck blood until they're about to burst.** Then they're off.

- **Why are cemeteries called "bone yards"?** During the Black Plague in Europe, graves weren't always six feet deep. When there was a storm, bony body parts could become exposed.

Trouble Sleeping?

Join the Club

Zzzzzzz

"There ain't no way to find out why a snorer can't hear himself snore."
—Mark Twain

It's the night before the first day of school. You're in bed under the covers. You close your eyes and listen to the older kids still playing outside. You open your eyes and watch the dwindling sunlight peeking through the edges of your window shade. You start to think about tomorrow: catching the school bus, deciding who to sit next to in the cafeteria, gym class.

You look at the clock. It's been a half hour since you got into bed. You've tossed, you've turned, and you feel more awake than ever.

What now?

Instead of doing what's natural — bouncing up and down on the box springs — you need to relax. It's perfectly normal to have trouble sleeping the night before a big day. It happens to people all over the world.

But if you have trouble getting to sleep every night, you have a problem. That's called **insomnia.**

There are close to 100 different disorders, insomnia included, that affect the amount and quality of the sleep we get. You've probably heard of some, like snoring and sleepwalking. Others are less common, but more serious.

Our muscles relax when we sleep. That's so while you're dreaming about playing against Monica Seles in the final round at Wimbledon, you don't knock over the lamp beside your bed.

But when you have **sleep apnea**, the muscles in your throat relax too much, so you can't breathe regularly. This occurs mainly in overweight men and is marked by loud snoring and a pause as long as a minute between breaths. Sleep apnea can often be cured by losing weight, but in more serious cases, surgery is required to cut away what doctors call the "excess mucosal folds" inside the throat to make the airway bigger.

6 FAMOUS INSOMNIACS

Mark Twain, author

While staying over a friend's house, Twain got so frustrated with his inability to sleep that he threw his pillow at a window. Pleased to notice a fresh breeze flowing through the room, Twain slept soundly that night. The next morning he determined he had smashed the window.

Marlene Dietrich, actress

You've heard a glass of warm milk helps when you're having trouble falling asleep. But what about Dietrich's solution: a sardine and onion sandwich on rye bread? Bet you'd prefer to count sheep.

W.C. Fields, actor

This noted insomniac made trying to get some shut-eye an adventure. Places he decided to sleep include a barber's chair, under an umbrella sprayed by a garden hose,

King of the Snorers

The loudest recorded snore blared out of Mark Thompson Hebbard in Vancouver, Canada. On November 3, 1987, a meter placed two feet above his head registered 90 decibels. Vancouver's traffic laws prohibit noise louder than 80 decibels.

and on a pool table. May we suggest the bed?

Judy Garland, actress and singer

Judy Garland was no normal teenager. By the time she turned 17, she'd not only starred as Dorothy in *The Wizard of Oz*, she'd become addicted to the pills her doctors gave her to stay thin. The drugs would keep her up three or four nights in a row. As a result, Garland started to take sleeping pills. She died at the age of 47, most probably of a drug overdose.

Groucho Marx, comedian

Groucho's sleeping troubles started the night of the Stock Market Crash of 1929, when he lost $240,000. That big mustache couldn't have made hitting the pillow any easier.

Amy Lowell, poet

Because she was so easily disturbed at night, Lowell would rent five rooms when she stayed at a hotel. Aside from the room she stayed in, she would get a room above and below and to either side. All on a poet's salary!

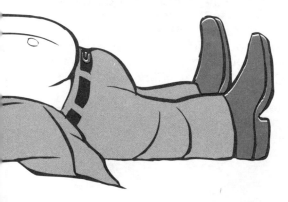

SLEEP PROBLEMS
YOU'D RATHER AVOID

Tooth-gnashing is just what it sounds like. Twenty percent of us do it in our sleep, either because we're stressed out or because our teeth need to be worked on by a dentist. If you grind or gnash at night, there's a simple solution that's supposed to work 75 percent of the time. Close your mouth and bite down slowly until your upper and lower teeth touch. Then count to five. Repeat this every few hours and you might solve the problem.

One in 100 of us suffer from **narcolepsy**. A narcoleptic falls asleep without warning, which can be dangerous while driving, messy while eating. And it doesn't matter how much sleep a narcoleptic gets. The only way to solve the most severe cases is to go to a doctor and get special medicine designed to help a narcoleptic stay awake.

Delayed Sleep Phase Syndrome has such a long name it is usually called DSPS. People with DSPS have trouble falling asleep at a regular hour. Then, because they are awake until at least midnight, people with DSPS struggle to get up the following morning. The problem can be traced to our body's timing system, known as our biological clock. That's right, each of us has a little clock somewhere inside our brain to tell us when to sleep, wake up, and take the chocolate chip cookies out of the oven. (Okay. That last part is an exaggeration.)

I'VE GOT RHYTHM

Circadian rhythms run our body clocks. For some reason our biological clock is on a 25-hour shift. That means if we didn't have sunlight, alarm clocks, and our parents to wake us up, we would get to sleep and get up one hour later than the night before. This could get pretty inconvenient. For example, if all we had were our body clocks, we would get up for school at 7 A.M. on Monday, 8 A.M. on Tuesday, and so on until we were waking up on Friday at 11 A.M.

Next time you're late for school, try telling this to the principal: "It wasn't my fault. My circadian rhythms got in the way."

Expensive, Expensive

Sleep problems cost $70 billion a year in lost productivity, industrial accidents, and medical bills, according to the Institute for Circadian Physiology in Boston.

A Nation of Sleepy-heads

What most adults want more than anything — no matter what they tell you — is to get more sleep. In a perfect world, stockbrokers would toss alarm clocks into garbage disposals, schoolteachers would scoot under their desks for afternoon naps, and doctors would slide under the covers on a warm summer evening for a full night of shut-eye.

Tired Americans have one man to blame. In 1880, Thomas Edison perfected the electric light. That was all it took to throw our body clocks for a permanent loop. You know the tired feeling you get if you take an airplane from one time zone to another? Studies have shown that turning on bright lights at night can disrupt our internal clocks as much as flying from New York to California several times.

Artificial light keeps us awake long past when our pre-Edison ancestors would be snoozing. College students have a particular problem turning out the lights. They don't reach their circadian nadir — the deep moment of sleep when body temperature is lowest — until 6:30 in the morning. Before electric lights, the circadian nadir occurred between midnight and 2 A.M.

The 22 million Americans who work through the night struggle the most with sleep problems. These are bakers, pilots, nurses, sailors, and telephone operators. They get only 5.6 hours of sleep each night.

Yawning: How Come?

We yawn because our oxygen intake, for whatever reason, has fallen below what our bodies require. A yawn is a deeper breath that allows us to take in more air than usual. It happens when we're bored or tired. There is no scientific reason that yawning seems to spread throughout a room, but some observers say it is simply that humans influence one another through the power of suggestion. If we see someone who is scared, we also become afraid. Yawning is contagious through the power of suggestion. You may be yawning right now, just reading this.

So why do we cover a yawn? To be polite, of course. The original custom, though, grew out of a fear that in one giant yawn, the soul might depart the body. A hand over the lips protected us from this life-sucking evil.

The Birth of
Teddy Bear
Nation

Imagine a world without Teddy Bears. Well, if you said the words 'teddy bear' out loud in 1894, you'd probably get the same looks someone today might receive if he or she kept talking about 'zargot munderpeels.'

See, there's no such thing as 'zargot munderpeels.' And until 1902, there was no such thing as a teddy bear.

The name came from Theodore Roosevelt, a popular president who happened to have a big mustache that made him look like a walrus.

Roosevelt loved to hunt. Sure enough, while negotiating a boundary dispute in Mississippi, the president took a break to go looking for bears. He came upon a baby cub and decided not to shoot. Good thinking, Mr. President: he posed near the cute bear for a newspaper photographer, and the picture made him even more popular. It inspired Morris Michtom, a toy store owner in Brooklyn, to make his own stuffed bear. Only minutes after displaying it in the window, someone bought the bear. So he made another. And another.

Michton wrote Roosevelt, asking permission to make more bears and use the president's name. No problema, the president said. Not a bad deal for Michton: a new product and the glowing endorsement of the president of the United States.

Try getting the president's approval today to sell a product bearing the presidential name. Trust us, Clinton Car Cleaner wouldn't get the commander-in-chief's endorsement.

By 1905, teddy bears had become the craze. They became so popular a priest spoke out against them. He feared that little girls who had abandoned dolls for bears would lose the instincts of motherhood. Yeah, right.

The president never tired of the fad, posing with teddy bears the rest of his life. When he died, Michton's son donated one of the very first bears to the Roosevelt estate.

FROM TOILET PAPER TO CRACKER JACKS

Some Inventions

• Waste Wizardry

The bathroom:
  8000 B.C., Scotland
Flushing toilet: 1775, England
Toilet paper: 1857,
  United States
Kleenex tissues: 1924,
  United States
Toothbrush: 3000 B.C., Egypt
Toothpaste: 2000 B.C., Egypt
Razor: 20,000 years ago, Asia and Africa
Shampoo: 1890s, Germany
Soap: 600 B.C. (Made by boiling goat
fat, water, and ash.)

• Let the Games Begin

Marbles: 3000 B.C., Egypt
Hula Hoop: 1000 B.C., Near East
Yo-Yo: 1000 B.C., China
Kite: 1200 B.C., China
Frisbee: Pre-1957, Connecticut
Teddy Bear: 1902, United States
Crossword Puzzle: 1913, New York
Board Games: 3000 B.C.,
  Mesopotamia
Parcheesi: 1570s, India
Monopoly: 1933, Pennsylvania
Scrabble: 1931, New England
Silly Putty: 1940s, Connecticut

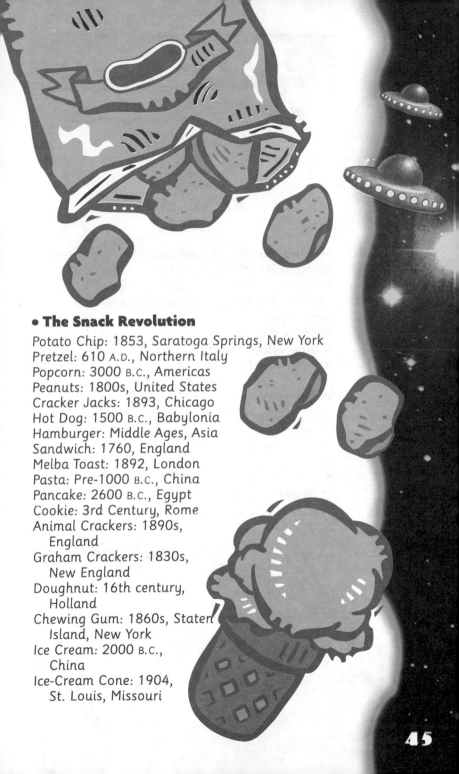

• The Snack Revolution

Potato Chip: 1853, Saratoga Springs, New York
Pretzel: 610 A.D., Northern Italy
Popcorn: 3000 B.C., Americas
Peanuts: 1800s, United States
Cracker Jacks: 1893, Chicago
Hot Dog: 1500 B.C., Babylonia
Hamburger: Middle Ages, Asia
Sandwich: 1760, England
Melba Toast: 1892, London
Pasta: Pre-1000 B.C., China
Pancake: 2600 B.C., Egypt
Cookie: 3rd Century, Rome
Animal Crackers: 1890s, England
Graham Crackers: 1830s, New England
Doughnut: 16th century, Holland
Chewing Gum: 1860s, Staten Island, New York
Ice Cream: 2000 B.C., China
Ice-Cream Cone: 1904, St. Louis, Missouri

Night Jokes

HORRIFY YOUR FAMILY BY TELLING THESE

☛ **Why** was the football player always tired in the morning? ◆ He couldn't stop sleepblocking.

☛ **Why** did the baker leave a loaf out in the rain? ◆ He'd always wanted to sleep on a waterbread.

☛ **How** does a cow ignore her alarm clock? ◆ By pressing the Moos button.

☛ **What** do you call a sleeping monster who just won't keep quiet? ◆ Frankensnore.

☛ **What** do you call a Grizzly who needs a nightlight in his cave? ◆ Beared of the dark.

☛ **Why** did the bed-bug stay home every night? ◆ He was an itchrovert.

☛ **Who** makes movies and sleeps late? ◆ Tom Snooze.

☛ **What** does a frog take when he goes camping? ◆ A tent, a flashlight, and a leaping bag.

ROCK STARS

They're NOT Like You and Me

DID YOU KNOW . . . ?

Alanis Morrisette was a teenage actress on Nickelodeon's "You Can't Do That on Television."

Bob Dylan's favorite games are Chess and Hearts.

Tina Turner's real name is Annie Mae Bullock.

Bobby Brown looks at a person's shoes the first time he meets someone. "If the shoes are neat, it says this person takes care of himself."

Madonna was a Campfire Girl and a Brownie.

James Brown likes to watch "60 Minutes."

Brian Wilson of the Beach Boys built a sandbox in his living room and put his piano in it.

Aretha Franklin subscribes to "Architectural Digest."

Neil Young wishes he could have been photographed with the ancient Egyptians building a pyramid behind him. (Some rock stars don't understand they didn't have cameras back then. Or rock stars!)

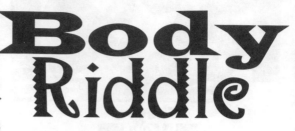

Body Riddle

Figure This One Out

Can you name nine body parts that are spelled with three letters each? Write your answers into the spaces provided.

Clue #1: One hangs on either side, and it rhymes with where Old McDonald had to reside.

☐☐☐

Clue #2: If you didn't have these, you'd never get far. You need 'em to walk, run, and drive a car.

☐☐☐

Clue #3: You can lick 'em when they're dry, or bend 'em in a smile. And when you go out dancing, paint 'em red for style.

☐☐☐

Clue #4: If you don't walk slow, you're gonna stub your _____ .

☐☐☐

Clue #5: There are blue ones, green ones, brown ones, too. And if you keep them closed, you'll sleep the whole day through.

☐☐☐

Clue #6: Have you heard about a painter named Vincent Van Gogh? He fell in love but she wouldn't be near, so he took a big knife and sliced off his _____ .

Clue #7: Only chew the kind you buy in a candy store. Otherwise your mouth is going to get bloody and sore.

Clue #8: Chomp, chomp, chomp. You use these to chew, or to name a big shark.

Clue #9: You'll need to shake 'em to rock.

Finished? Now use the following letters to form a two-word answer:

The second letter in the answer to Clue #1.
The first letter in the answer to Clue #2.
The second letter in the answer to Clue #3.
The first letter in the answer to Clue #4.
The second letter in the answer to Clue #5.
The first letter in the answer to Clue #6.
The first letter in the answer to Clue #7.
The second letter in the answer to Clue #8.
The first letter in the answer to Clue #9.

Need help?
Here's a clue to what the two words should spell out: if you're beaming bright, it very well might take you this long to travel 5,800,000,000,000 miles. If you're stumped, see the astronomy Dextionary on pages 30 and 31.

The unscrambled word should spell out: light year
Leg, Lip, **G**um, **H**ip, **T**oe, **E**ye, Ear, J**A**w, A**R**m

Answers to the clues: 1. arm; 2. leg; 3. lip; 4. toe; 5. eye; 6. ear; 7. gum; 8. jaw; 9. hip.

49

Musical
I·N·T·E·R·L·U·D·E

Four Weird Instruments

◆ The Appolonicon was played in England and sounded like an orchestra due to its five separate keyboards.

◆ The Pantaleon, which had 276 strings and stretched 11 feet long, was the largest string instrument ever made for a single player.

◆ The Guitarpa was part violin-cello (3 strings), part guitar (6 strings), and part harp (26 strings).

◆ The Panomonico was comprised of 378 instruments, including 150 flutes, 50 oboes, and 18 trumpets.

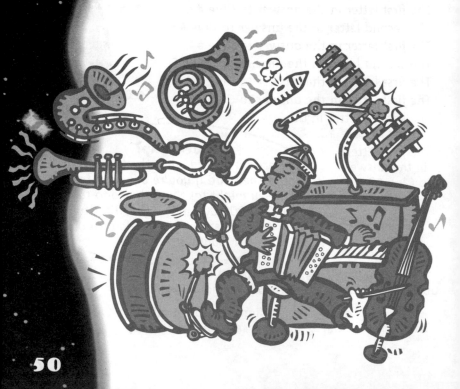

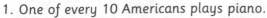

Piano Talk

True or false?

1. One of every 10 Americans plays piano.
2. The first piano was built by cavemen with dinosaur tusks.
3. At a 1904 convention of piano manufacturers, a group of old pianos was burned as part of a ceremony for the new, upright models.
4. A tiny trained monkey lives inside player pianos.
5. Liberace once made $138,000 for a single show.

Answers:
1. true; 2. false; 3. true; 4. false; 5. true.

Out of Control

The record for continuous piano playing is held by Heinz Arntz. He played 1,056 hours straight — except for two hours of sleep for each of the 44 days of his streak.

THE 10 MOST POPULAR INSTRUMENTS			
Instrument	Played by this percent of people	This percent of males play it	This percent of females play it
piano	34%	17%	50%
guitar	22%	36%	8%
drums	6%	11%	1%
flute	5%	2%	8%
organ	4%	1%	7%
alto saxophone	4%	5%	3%
keyboard	4%	4%	4%
clarinet	4%	1%	6%
trumpet	3%	6%	1%
violin	3%	2%	4%

SOME FIRSTS

Mind Your Manners

The first mention of childhood manners appeared in 1530 in a book by Dutch author Erasmus. His advice?

1. If you're having trouble swallowing a piece of food, turn around discreetly and toss it somewhere.

2. Vomit if you must, but always remember it's less objectionable to vomit all over the road than to keep that vomit in your throat.

3. Don't move around in your chair. This gives the impression you're farting.

4. Don't offer someone else your handkerchief unless it was recently washed. After you wipe your nose, don't stare into the handkerchief as if the Crown Jewels fell out of your head.

Forkless Rules

Before the first fork was introduced in the 11th century, people ate with their hands. But there were rules. Common folk grabbed the grub with five fingers; the upper-class eater lifted it daintily, with three fingers. The food was never to touch the ring finger or pinkie.

The Toilet Paper Environmentalists of 1857

When toilet paper was first introduced in 1857, Americans wouldn't use it. Naturally, they wanted instead to make full use of the old department store catalogs and newspapers hanging around the house.

Tooth Roots

The first toothbrush was a pencil-sized stick dating back to 3000 B.C. The first bristle toothbrush was made in China in 1498. The bristles were plucked from the backs of hogs living in the cold sections of China and Siberia. Nylon bristle toothbrushes were introduced in America in 1938.

Paste, Too

Toothpaste was created by Egyptian physicians 4,000 years ago. It was made of powdered vinegar and pumice, and was a lot better than early Roman toothpaste, which happened to be made from human urine. First-century Roman physicians maintained that brushing with urine whitened teeth and fixed them more firmly into the gums.

Dream Dream Dream

We Dream 1,600 Times a Year!

There are two kinds of sleep: REM and non-REM sleep. Neither has a thing to do with music. REM stands for rapid eye movement. Because when we sleep, our eyes move like crazy.

Watch someone sleeping. (Get permission first, of course.) Pay attention to the bulge of the eyeballs under the eyelids. If the bulges move rapidly, that person is most likely in REM sleep.

But Why Don't We Thrash Around More?

Say you're having a dream about running around at recess and someone in the dream throws a medicine ball at you. You catch it in your dream, but in real life, don't move at all. Why? Just as you start to dream, your brain relaxes all your muscles so you won't thrash around. But you do move around a little. Ever see a dog or cat twitch when sleeping? That's because of dreaming.

Your Brain, the Computer

When we dream, our minds work like computers. They consider what our choices are in life and organize messages to broadcast only during a dream. To most of us, this adds up to a meaningless group of symbols that make no sense. You might wake up and remember being on an island and having an Oreo cookie on your foot. Not very helpful, is it?

Dreams Can Be Useful

In the late 1800s, the German scientist Friedrich Kekuthle dreamed of a snake swallowing its tail. This somehow told him that benzene molecules consist of closed rings. Make sense? Of course not. That's why he's a German scientist.

Satisfaction Guaranteed

Keith Richards, the guitarist for the Rolling Stones, dreamed up the music for the song, "(I Can't Get No) Satisfaction." He kept a tape recorder by his bed. One morning, he discovered he'd hummed the tune that would make him rich and famous. He'd also snored for the remainder of the tape.

A Dream Come TRUE

SEVERAL EXAMPLES OF WHAT THE NIGHT CAN DO

Devil Music

When he was just 21, Italian violinist Giuseppe Tartini dreamed he had sold his soul to the devil. But boy could Satan play! In the dream, Tartini handed the horned one his violin and listened to one of the most beautiful pieces he had ever heard. When he woke up, Tartini tried to recreate the piece, but couldn't. Still, he considered the work he came up with — the Devil's Sonata — his best.

Archaeological Assistance

In 1893, German archaeologist Hermann V. Hilprecht was struggling to understand what had been written, in the ancient language of cuneiform, on two tiny fragments from Babylon. Stumped, Hilprecht went to bed. He was visited in a dream by a tall priest who told him the pieces were part of a larger set, and explained what was written on them. The next morning, when Hilprecht returned to his work, he found that it all made perfect sense. The 3,000-year-old tablet was called the Stone of Nebuchadnezzar.

Dream Poet

In the middle of a nice, summer afternoon in 1797, Samuel Taylor Coleridge dozed off while he was reading a book about the 13th century Mongol emperor, Kubla Khan. The lines for a poem came to him in the dream, and when he woke up, Coleridge began to write furiously. He got to the 54th line when a visitor arrived. By the time the man had left, Coleridge had forgotten the rest of the lines. "Kubla Kahn," published in 1816, would be his most famous work.

Dog Vacuum

As strange as it may sound, there is a product called Dog-Done, which sucks prairie dogs — rodents living mainly in the west — out of their burrows into a large tank where they can be taken somewhere out of the way of crops. Gay Balfour, who is from Colorado, got the idea in a dream. "I saw a large yellow vehicle and there were green hoses running from it. I was putting the hoses in the ground, sucking out prairie dogs."

Thanks, Shammy

In ancient Sumeria, dreams were believed to be messages from Shamash, the sun god.

Deep Thinking

"The best way to get your dreams to come true is to wake up."—Paul Valéry

Hey: Keep a Dream Log

The writer Jack Kerouac published a book of his dreams.

Comedian and songwriter Steve Allen always keeps a pencil and pad at his bedside. His biggest hit song came to him in a dream.

Don't feel that you have to compete with that, but, just for fun, let's see what happens when you try to keep track of your dreams.

You will need only a pad of paper, pencil, and spot near your bed to keep your dream log.

The instructions are simple: whenever you wake up and remember a dream, write it down. The characters, the plot, the weird things that happened. Do the best you can to keep track of the date.

Check the notebook the next morning. Is there a connection between what happened during the day and what you dreamed? Are the same people showing up night after night? Or is it all just a random sampling of unrelated ideas and people you haven't seen for a long time?

No matter what the dreams are like, hold onto the log. Those dreams belong to you.

DAYTIME NIGHTMARES

A CRAFTY PLAN

You need the following: cooked spaghetti, spaghetti sauce, corn flakes, peeled grapes, raisins, and apple sauce. Call a friend into the room, have that friend close both eyes and hold out a hand. Then put each item, one at a time, into his hand and tell your friend what he's really holding.

Put in hand:	Say that it's:
grape	eyeball
cooked spaghetti	intestines
cooked spaghetti and sauce	bloody intestines
corn flakes	scabs
raisins	boogers
raisins and apple sauce	wet boogers

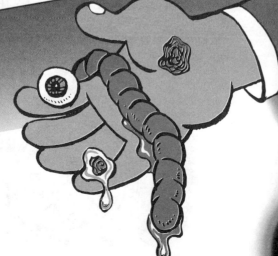

THE *Idiom* ADVANTAGE

What do the terms, "bury the hatchet," "cry over spilt milk," and "go off the deep end" have in common? They are all idioms — expressions that don't make sense if you take them literally, but make you look smart when you use them in the right situation.

For example, if you're running for president and the poll results show your opponent leading by 14 points, you're "down in the dumps." If you're playing hide-and-seek and end up hiding behind a tree that's too narrow, you're a "sitting duck." And when your cousin Larry tries to convince you he's been asked to play second base for the Atlanta Braves, it's safe to say that he's "pulling your leg."

The word *idiom* comes from the Greek root, *idio.* It means "unique signature." Idioms are great fun. They only make sense in the language they are spoken. If you need proof, find someone who speaks French to translate two popular idioms: "birthday suit" and "under the weather."

Here are a few of the most common idioms and what they mean:

Idiom	Meaning	Example
all thumbs	clumsy or awkward	"Herman tried to juggle the flaming knives, but he was all thumbs and ended up slicing off his ears."
beat around the bush	avoid getting to the point	"Instead of beating around the bush, Shelly told her dad she accidentally poured a glass of apple juice over his computer."
cry over spilt milk	dwell on mistakes	"You regret buying Alanis Morrisette's album, but there's no use crying over spilt milk."
eat crow	admit to having been wrong	"Millicent promised her parents she would always get straight A's, but she had to eat crow when they saw the C's on her report card."

take it with a grain of salt	not take it very seriously	"Lauren knew her hair cut was horrible, so whenever people told her she looked foxy, she took it with a grain of salt."
make no bones about it	be blunt and candid	"Mr. Sanders made no bones about it: He likes to give pop quizzes, and his math class better be ready."
play it by ear	not plan ahead of time	"Curtis decided to wait until after dinner to ask what movie Cindy cared to see. It was their first date, and he wanted to play it by ear."
take the cake	do it the best	"When it comes to chewing her gum like a cow, Sara really takes the cake."

Sleep WALKING

If you have ever walked in your sleep, you have company. Four million Americans have sought help for sleepwalking, according to the American Medical Association. About 10 to 15 percent of children sleepwalk, and about 5 percent of all American adults do.

We sleepwalk when we are tense or anxious. And when we sleepwalk, our brains are only half awake. This can lead to some interesting problems.

Question: What happens when your brain is awake enough to tell you how to walk down the hallway, but too asleep to tell you when there's a wall in your way?

Answer: You walk into that wall.

Gross

The average heart pumps between 50 and 60 million gallons of blood over a lifetime. That's 66 gallons an hour, and 1.1 gallons a minute. The average human heart weighs 10 ounces. (A pound is 16 ounces.) A whale caught in 1947 had a heart weighing 1,540 pounds.

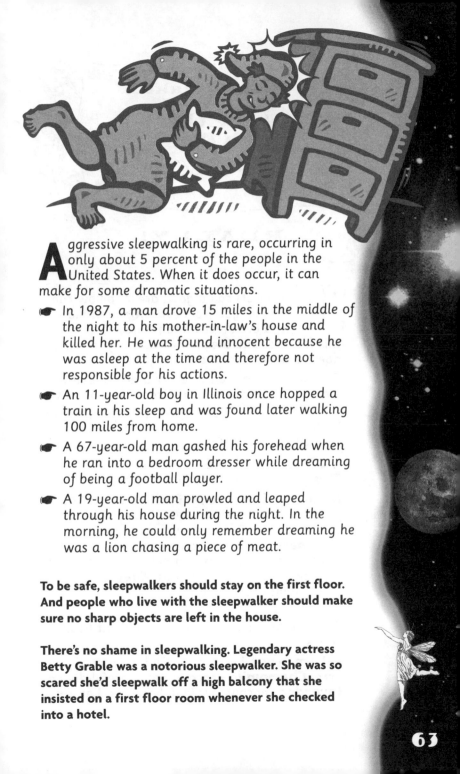

Aggressive sleepwalking is rare, occurring in only about 5 percent of the people in the United States. When it does occur, it can make for some dramatic situations.

☞ In 1987, a man drove 15 miles in the middle of the night to his mother-in-law's house and killed her. He was found innocent because he was asleep at the time and therefore not responsible for his actions.

☞ An 11-year-old boy in Illinois once hopped a train in his sleep and was found later walking 100 miles from home.

☞ A 67-year-old man gashed his forehead when he ran into a bedroom dresser while dreaming of being a football player.

☞ A 19-year-old man prowled and leaped through his house during the night. In the morning, he could only remember dreaming he was a lion chasing a piece of meat.

To be safe, sleepwalkers should stay on the first floor. And people who live with the sleepwalker should make sure no sharp objects are left in the house.

There's no shame in sleepwalking. Legendary actress Betty Grable was a notorious sleepwalker. She was so scared she'd sleepwalk off a high balcony that she insisted on a first floor room whenever she checked into a hotel.

How To Make A
Dream Pillow

REALLY!

Herbalists say a good dream pillow can protect you from evil, stop nightmares, and even reveal the future. They say this for a reason: they're herbalists. If this stuff doesn't work, they're out of a job.

The jury's still out on whether a dream pillow makes a difference in your sleep world. But even if it just smells funny, a dream pillow is good fun to make.

Here's how:

1. GET SOME HERBS

These should be easy to find at grocery stores:

Anise - prevents dreams. **Basil** - protects you from evil. **Cloves** - gives you dreams with a clear message. **Dill** - puts babies to sleep. **Rosemary** - helps you keep away evil dreams. **Sage** - induces trances and aids dream journeys. **Thyme** - helps you see fairies. **Oregano** - gives you a night of calm sleep.

These herbs are most likely available at health stores:

Balsam - cures heartaches. **Cedar** - a purifying herb. **Chamomile** - encourages peaceful dreams. **Lavender** - encourages joyful dreams. **Lemon**

balm - *calms and relaxes.* **Mint** - *cures headaches.*
Mugwort - *encourages vivid, wild dreams.*
Mullein - *protects against nightmares.*
Peppermint - *encourages sleep and dreams of the future.* **Roses** - *creates restful sleep and sweet, pleasant dream.* **Sandalwood** - *helps healing.*

2. MAKE A PILLOW COVER

You need a piece of fabric — anything from a corduroy patch to part of an old cotton shirt. First, cut out a round or square piece from this cloth. That is what you'll be stuffing with herbs. You can make your piece as small as the bottom of a coffee can or as large as a dinner plate. If you don't like sewing, you'll only need one piece of fabric to make the pillow. Otherwise, cut off two.

3. MAKE HERB PILLOW STUFFING

Take some of your herbs and place them in the center of the fabric. To avoid sewing, fold the dream pillow and tie it at the top with string or a ribbon. If you want to sew, put the two fabric pieces together and sew about two-thirds of the way around the edges. Make sure to leave an opening big enough to drop the herb stuffing through. Once the pillow has been stuffed, sew up the remaining third.

**Q: What's soft, smells like a pizza, and helps you sleep?
A: A pillow full of oregano!**

Beware: some herbs are awfully strong. If you want a dream pillow without an overwhelming scent, try mixing cloth or nylon or clean rags into the center of the soon-to-be-folded fabric.

There you go. A Dream Pillow. Now the big question: does it work?

SKATEBOARD MANIA

How much do you really know about America's legendary asphalt surfboards? To find out, try this quiz.

1. Skateboards were first spotted in Belgium in the 1750s.
True   False

2. At one time, New Jersey, New York, and Massachusetts had all banned skateboards from major roads.
True   False

3. The first skateboards marketed across the country were made of ivory, not wood.
True   False

4. The most famous skateboarder in Hollywood was Zsa Zsa Gabor, whose board was lined with tiny diamonds.
True   False

5. Boards became safer in the 1970s when the government required all users to seek a license to operate. The test included backing your board into a tight parking space.
True   False

Answers: 1. T; 2. T; 3. F; 4. F; 5. F; 6. T; 7. F; 8. T; 9. T; 10. F.

6. The "Coffin" move calls for a skateboarder to lie flat on his or her back on the board, arms folded across the chest.

True   **False**

7. The International Olympic Committee sanctioned skateboarding as a tentative trial sport for the year 2000.

True   **False**

8. The California Medical Association called skateboarding a "medical menace" when it started to become popular in the 1960s.

True   **False**

9. Skateboards were used during World War II when there was a shortage of gasoline. Many workers used the boards to get to and from work.

True   **False**

10. The record for skateboard jumping is 32 cars, set by Jumpy Joe Willikers in 1947.

True

False

IT'S NOT EASY BEING A FAD

Fads are fashions that become popular very quickly. Pogs are a fad. So are Power Rangers and Roller Blades. Some fads — like bell-bottoms and drag races — fade away. Others — like television and rock 'n' roll — remain as strong as ever.

Because they are thrust upon us so fast, fads often alarm some members of society. In other words, new things scare people. This can lead those people to say some pretty funny stuff. The following five quotes were spoken soon after a fad began. Can you guess which fad the quotes refer to?

1. "The tailor, the hatter, the booksellers, the shoemaker, the horse dealer, and the riding master all tell similar tales of woe."

   a. bicycles **b.** badminton **c.** rubber

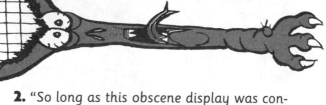

2. "So long as this obscene display was confined to prostitutes and adulteresses, we did not think it deserving of notice; but now that it is attempted to be forced upon the respectable classes, we feel it a duty to warm every parent against exposing his daughter to so fatal a contagion."

   a. mini-skirts **b.** rock 'n' roll **c.** the waltz

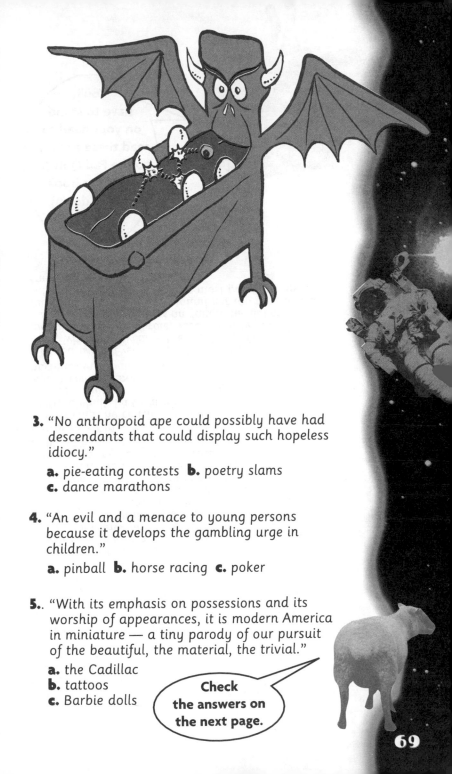

3. "No anthropoid ape could possibly have had descendants that could display such hopeless idiocy."

   a. pie-eating contests **b.** poetry slams
   c. dance marathons

4. "An evil and a menace to young persons because it develops the gambling urge in children."

   a. pinball **b.** horse racing **c.** poker

5.. "With its emphasis on possessions and its worship of appearances, it is modern America in miniature — a tiny parody of our pursuit of the beautiful, the material, the trivial."

   a. the Cadillac
   b. tattoos
   c. Barbie dolls

Check the answers on the next page.

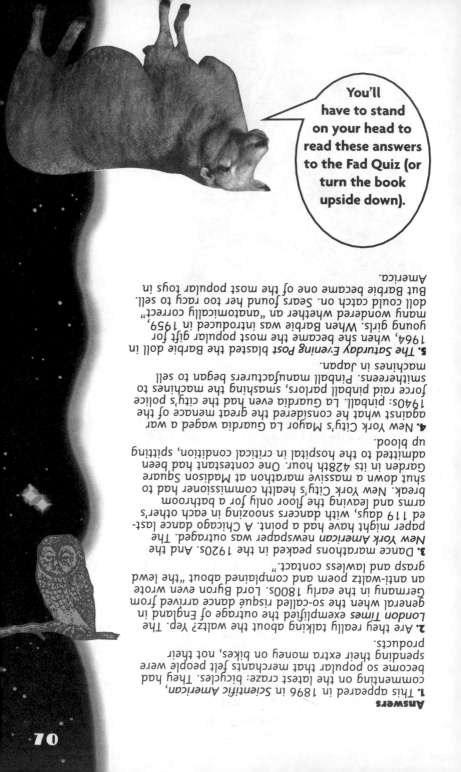

You'll have to stand on your head to read these answers to the Fad Quiz (or turn the book upside down).

Answers

1. This appeared in 1896 in *Scientific American*, commenting on the latest craze: bicycles. They had become so popular that merchants felt people were spending their extra money on bikes, not their products.

2. Are they really talking about the waltz? Yep. The *London Times* exemplified the outrage of England in general when the so-called risqué dance arrived from Germany in the early 1800s. Lord Byron even wrote an anti-waltz poem and complained about "the lewd grasp and lawless contact."

3. Dance marathons peaked in the 1920s. And the *New York American* newspaper was outraged. The paper might have had a point. A Chicago dance lasted 119 days, with dancers snoozing in each other's arms and leaving the floor only for a bathroom break. New York City's health commissioner had to shut down a massive marathon at Madison Square Garden in its 428th hour. One contestant had been admitted to the hospital in critical condition, spitting up blood.

4. New York City's Mayor La Guardia waged a war against what he considered the great menace of the 1940s: pinball. La Guardia even had the city's police force raid pinball parlors, smashing the machines to smithereens. Pinball manufacturers began to sell machines in Japan.

5. *The Saturday Evening Post* blasted the Barbie doll in 1964, when she became the most popular gift for young girls. When Barbie was introduced in 1959, many wondered whether an "anatomically correct" doll could catch on. Sears found her too racy to sell. But Barbie became one of the most popular toys in America.

Want to open your own McDonald's?

Start saving your allowance.

Here are the top franchises in America and the cost to open one location, according to *Entrepreneur* magazine. Bear in mind that an economics professor at Wayne State University determined that of the 21,000 franchises opened one recent year, 35 percent failed.

Name	They sell	Cost to open one
Subway	submarine sandwiches	$55,000 to $140,000
7-Eleven	convenience store stuff	$12,500
Burger King	the Whopper, etc.	$247,000 to $1.3 million
McDonald's	the Big Mac, etc.	$363,000 to $591,000
Dunkin' Donuts	what do you think?	$181,000 to $255,000
Baskin-Robbins	ice cream	$42,000 to $370,000

Did you know . . .

The McDonald's Filet-O-Fish sandwich debuted in 1963. It was created in response to Catholics in Cincinnati who couldn't eat meat on Fridays.

VEGETABLE NEWS YOU CAN USE

Garlic

You know it stinks, but did you know ...

• In Ancient Egypt, priests considered garlic dirty. You couldn't enter a temple with garlic on your breath.

• In Rome, soldiers ate garlic believing it gave them strength.

• In England, people rubbed garlic on a baby's lips to ward off vampires and witches. Yummy!

• In Asia, garlic is believed to be good for the complexion.

• In America, garlic was virtually ignored until the 20th century. Today, 20 million pounds of garlic are grown in the United States every year.

Asparagus

If it's the vegetable of the rich, why does it make your pee smell?

1. Asparagus has always been considered a luxury food. Cleopatra served it when she was entertaining, as did French King Louis XIV.
2. The word is based on the Latin for "sprout" and "shoot."
3. Thomas Jefferson, our third president, was one of the earliest asparagus farmers in America.
4. Asparagus is more expensive than almost any other vegetable.
5. Although it originated in Southern England and sections of Europe, more than 120,000 tons of asparagus are now grown in the United States.

Tomato

Once a fruit, now a vegetable.

1. Tomatoes are native to South and Central America and weren't introduced in Europe until the 1500s. They were called "Apples of Love" but feared by many as poisonous.
2. In 1893, a U.S. court ruled tomatoes a fruit if eaten alone or before a meal, a vegetable if eaten with a meal.
3. Tomato juice was first canned in America in 1929. Today, we drink 35 million cases of it a year. (Yech!)
4. The largest tomato ever weighed four and a half pounds and was grown in the British Isles.
5. Ketchup — which the Heinz company began selling in 1876 — is made from tomatoes, vinegar, salt, sugar, and spices.

THE NUMBERS TELL THE STORY

Average teacher salary
in Connecticut:
$49,800
in Idaho: $27,800

Houses with cable television
in 1980: 15 million
in 1994: 59 million

Personal computers sold
in United States: 14,775,000
in Western Europe and Asia: 16,723,202
in rest of the world: 7,344,798

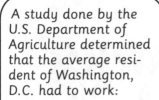

A study done by the U.S. Department of Agriculture determined that the average resident of Washington, D.C. had to work:

3 minutes for flour
4 minutes for a quart of whole milk
5 minutes for a dozen eggs
5 minutes for sugar
9 minutes for butter
18 minutes for cheddar cheese
21 minutes for a sirloin steak
30 minutes for coffee

Value of fur clothing sold
in 1982:
  $419,000,000
in 1992:
  $205,000,000

Supermarkets that accept credit cards
in 1990: 19 percent
in 1993: 51 percent

Gas stations
in California: 14,982
in Alaska: 281

SPARKS IN THE DARK

If you're looking for something

to do in the dark, we have a suggestion. Create your own light show. All right, so it's not going to be big enough to draw a crowd, but the cool thing is that all you need for the performance is a package of Wint-O-Green Life Savers, a dark room, and a friend.

Here's what you do:

1. Turn off the lights and talk to each other until your eyes adjust to the dark.

2. Put a Wint-O-Green Life Saver on your lower back teeth. (Try not to get too much gooey saliva on the candy.)

3. Chomp! Do it impolitely, with your mouth open, so everyone can see the candy being crushed.

Your friend should see blue sparks when the candy crushes. If not, try again. And then, when you've completed your performance, let your friend do some chomping. That way everybody gets a good show.

So why does it happen?

It's called triboluminescence. (Just try to repeat that out loud a few times.) Triboluminescence occurs when two materials crash into each other — in this case, the wintergreen flavoring (called methyl salicylate) and the sugar molecules.

If you don't believe us, we suggest you call Linda Sweeting. She's an organic chemist at Towson State University. In 1988, she presented a report on sparking Life Savers at a chemistry conference in Toronto.

And while we're on the subject, here are a few other facts you should know about America's most popular hard candy.

Clarence Crane, a chocolate manufacturer from Cleveland, invented Life Savers in 1912. He needed a temporary replacement for chocolate, which melted in the summer. In 1913, Crane sold his Life Saver business for only $2,900. He was sure the candy wouldn't catch on. By 1915, the New York advertising man who bought Life Savers was making $250,000 a year.

◆ There are 11 different rolls available. The most popular are: Five Flavor (orange, pineapple, wild cherry, lemon, and lime), Wint-O-Green, Pep-O-Mint, and Butter Rum. The least popular are: Tropical Fruits (fruit punch, pina colada, mango melon, tangerine, and banana), Chill-O-Mints (wintergreen, spearmint, vanilla mint, and peppermint), and Wild Sour Berries (strawberry, red raspberry, black raspberry, blackberry, and cherry berry).

◆ Nabisco, which owns Life Savers, has kept track of alternative uses for the candy, as reported by Life Saver devotees over the years. Life Savers can be used as a flavoring in hot tea, a cure for seasickness, Christmas tree ornaments, golf tees, and candle holders on a birthday cake. We have a suggestion of our own: dessert Cheerios.

◆ With 29.6 million pounds sold each year, Life Savers are tops among hard roll candy. The 2.9 million rolls of Life Savers produced every day would form a road stretching 74 miles. Unfortunately, that road would be extremely thin — about the width of a Life Saver.

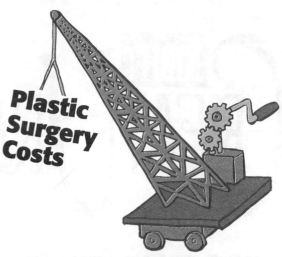

Plastic Surgery Costs

The best reason to stay away from any kind of cosmetic plastic surgery: it's expensive. If you want a tight stomach, we suggest a few sit-ups, not a tummy tuck.

Procedure	Average Cost
Butt lift	$3,084
Chemical peel (full face)	$1,634
Chemical peel (regional)	$ 682
Face lift	$4,156
Liposuction	$1,622
Hair plugs (single)	$ 101
Hair plugs (a strip)	$1,096
Nose job	$2,997
Tummy tuck	$3,618

Did you know . . .
A woman in Poughkeepsie, New York sued her plastic surgeon after he performed a tummy tuck on her. Claiming her belly-button was now 2 1/2 inches off center, she won $200,000 from the doctor.

NIGHT CREATURES

BEDTIME is supposed to be quiet time. At least that's what you would think from all the adults whispering "Shhh!" But for many living creatures, night is when everything gets busy. Have you ever noticed a cricket's chirp on a hot summer night? Or a raccoon knocking over a garbage can in search of yesterday's chicken wings? How about a wolf howling at the moon? And that's not all.

At least half the creatures on Earth are busy while we sleep. At night, these nocturnal animals emerge from the ground, their nests, and caves to hunt for food, hide from predators, and just hang out.

For animals that live near the desert, surviving the heat is often the difference between night and day. If they ran around when the sun was out, they would get sick and dehydrated. Same for most insects. That's why the best place to find worms is in the damp soil under a cold rock. For a worm, the bottom of a rock is better than the softest comforter.

There's another good reason many animals like the night. Us.

Humans are nice to have around when it's feeding time at the zoo, but in the wild, we usually do nothing but get in the way. We've built highways where deer once ran free. We've erected malls where wild horses used to roam. For nocturnal animals, night is almost like stepping into a time machine. Most humans are tucked under the covers.

The animals can take over.

81

BAT STUFF

Here's something you don't want to do: turn off all the lights in the house. Then try running as fast as you can. Ouch! — that's the kitchen table; ooops! — your sister's bureau; smash! — the bathroom sink.

If only you were a bat.

While humans need radar machines or special infra-red binoculars to see at night, bats have a special system that allows them to maneuver in the dark. It's called sonar and is built-in, like our senses of smell, sight, hearing, touch, and taste. As they fly, bats squeal, and the sonar picks up the noise bouncing off an upcoming object. Then the bats know to move before they whack into something.

Yes, vampire bats do exist. They have sharp front teeth to cut into flesh, and long tongues with which they lap and suck blood.

The good news is, most bats are not vampires.

The majority of bats eat fruit, insects, and even fish. And vampire bats don't usually attack humans. They swoop down on horses, cows, and chickens, sucking until their tiny bat stomachs are full of thick gobs of animal blood. Yum!

Most bats hang out in cool, dark caves. Some bats hang in unexpected places. The Asian bamboo bat sleeps in a stick of bamboo. The brown-nosed African bat sleeps in a porcupine burrow (ouch!). Woolly bats sometimes stop in a bird's nest for a nap. If you're a bird, this is bad news.

You've probably heard the idiom "Blind as a bat." From now on, your response should be simply, "Bats are not blind."

Bats have small eyes that are almost hidden by fur. But they work. The funny thing is that the bats with the best eyes — African bats — have the most trouble seeing at night. Sometimes they even run into telephone wires.

Bats do have one thing in common with humans, and it's not those beady eyes and hairy backs. When a bat wakes up and tries to fly too soon, it bumps into obstacles. If you see this happen, you might think to yourself, "That's one groggy bat."

The Natural Look

Bat poop was a key ingredient of eyeliner and mascara until recently.

OWLS BIG-TIME NIGHT SNACKER

If "blind as a bat" makes no sense, how can anyone with good conscience use the expression, "dog-eat-dog"? Everybody knows dogs don't eat dogs. They eat dog food!

The most accurate animal expression is "night owl." As in: "My Aunt Sadie stays up late. She's a real night owl."

Owls are birds that stay up all night to do more than hoot.

Night is when they eat breakfast, lunch, and dinner.

How do they do it? Owls have eyes that are 10 times more sensitive to light than ours. The eyes of some owls are so big they almost touch each other, which is actually a problem. Think about it. If your eyes took up half your head, where would everything else go? Big-eyed owls have no room for the muscles needed to make their eyes move. That's why they have to turn their necks to see something to the side.

Owls have very good ears. Great gray owls have been spotted diving into deep piles of snow to capture a mouse scurrying underneath.

Most owls eat everything from bugs and rabbits to snakes and mice. They have very bad table manners. Owls swallow their victim whole and spit out the indigestible parts as pellets. They don't use silverware, either.

Sssssssnakes

Hunters of the Night

Pit viper. Say that out loud a few times. Doesn't sound friendly, does it? Well, they aren't.

A pit viper is a snake with fangs so big they have to be folded like a lawn chair to fit inside its mouth. Venom pumps through these hollow fangs like water through a faucet. Except for one big difference. Venom kills. Some people have been poisoned even after a snake is dead by touching a fang by mistake. Venom, in fact, can be dangerous 50 years after the snake that produced it died.

Pit vipers hunt in total darkness. Instead of using their eyes, they are sensitive to movement, sounds, and heat.

Boas and pythons are not much nicer. The Cuban boa grows to 14 feet and likes to hunt for bats in caves. Talk about a midnight snack! The reticulated python and the anaconda are the longest snakes, some growing to be 30 feet long.

Large boa constrictors have been known to swallow crocodiles, deer, and even children. How, you might ask, does something as thin as a snake swallow something as wide as a deer? For one thing, boas have elastic, highly mobile jaws and well-developed salivary glands that help them lubricate their throats when swallowing. Imagine that. It's bad enough you're getting eaten alive by a snake; you have to be spit on, too!

Snake Fact
The krait, a highly venomous nocturnal snake, kills about 15,000 people a year in India. Krait venom is 40 times as dangerous as cyanide.

Life In The *Fast Lane*

Did you know that the cheetah, which can run 70 miles per hour, is the fastest animal on earth? The slowest is the snail, which needs 33 hours to go a single mile.

Here are some other animals and their speeds:

Animal	Miles per hour
Lion	50
Elk	45
Zebra	40
Hyena	40
Mongolian Wild Ass	40
Greyhound	39.35
Giraffe	32
Grizzly Bear	30
Cat	30
Human	27.89
Elephant	25
Pig	11
Chicken	9
Giant Tortoise	1.7
Three-toed Sloth	1.5

Big-Hearted

An elephant's heart can weigh as much as 35 pounds. And boy can elephants eat! A single elephant consumes 600 pounds of food a day, washing it down with 30 gallons of water.

WHICH BOOK IS NOT LIKE THE OTHERS?

The staff at the New York Public Library put together a list of books that shaped the 20th century. Can you pick the book in each category that doesn't belong?

Landmarks of Modern Literature
a. Anton Chekhov,
The Three Sisters
b. Franz Kafka,
The Metamorphosis
c. Carrie O. Key,
My Life as a Toll-Taker
d. Toni Morrison,
Song of Solomon
e. Virginia Woolf,
To the Lighthouse

Nature's Realm
a. Albert Einstein,
The Meaning of Relativity
b. Edward O. Wilson,
The Diversity of Life
c. Aldo Leopold,
A Sand County Almanac
d. Rush Limbaugh, The
Trees Are Justa Crop
e. Rachel Carson,
Silent Spring

Protest & Progress
a. John Steinbeck,
The Grapes of Wrath
b. W.E.B. Du Bois,
The Souls of Black Folk
c. Upton Sinclair,
The Jungle
d. Harriet Sugarhead,
*The Great Pez Dispenser
Strike of '79*
e. Randy Shilts,
And The Band Played On

Popular Culture
a. Joseph Heller, *Catch-22*
b. Bram Stoker, *Dracula*
c. Beverly Hills 90210,
More Than Words
d. Raymond Chandler,
The Big Sleep
e. Nathanael West,
The Day of the Locust

Women Writers
a. Edith Wharton,
The Age of Innocence
b. Zora Neale Hurston,
Dust Tracks on a Road
c. Betty Friedan,
*The Feminine
Mystique*
d. Alice Walker,
The Color Purple
e. Nancy Reagan,
*The
Unauthorized
Biography,*
Kitty Kelley

Answers:
1. c; 2. d; 3. d; 4. c; 5. e.

The Night SHIFT

Folks Who Work When the Sun Don't Shine

Bats, owls, and snakes aren't the only creatures working at night. In case you hadn't noticed, there are millions of humans who also burn the midnight oil. At 3 A.M. each morning, the number of Americans awake and working peaks at 10 million — as much as the combined populations of Mongolia, New Zealand, and Norway.

Who are these people?

They're truckers, construction workers, policemen, radio talk show hosts, taxi drivers, telephone operators, newspaper reporters, emergency room doctors, and convenience store workers.

- At Dunkin Donuts University, just south of Boston, students work in shifts between 1 A.M. and 9 A.M. to learn how to bake jelly doughnuts, crullers, and chocolate glazed munchkins properly.
- In New York City, stock market traders are hard at work when the sun goes down. Remember, midnight in Manhattan is two o'clock in the afternoon in Tokyo. A perfect time to make money.

A Cop Talks

Police Officer Paul Burke works the midnight-to-8 A.M. shift in Cambridge, Massachusetts. He stepped off the beat for a few minutes to talk about working at night.

Q: Do police officers really eat doughnuts?
A: No. I can't say that. I probably eat a half dozen doughnuts a year. Very rarely do I eat a

doughnut. My partner never eats doughnuts. My partner doesn't even drink coffee. The trend now is for people to be healthier and be conscious of what they eat. You can't even smoke if you were hired after 1988. Police, like everyone else, are more conscious of what they eat, drink, and put in their systems.

Q: Why do police officers wear blue?
A: Police officers wear blue mostly for concealment at night, so you can blend in with the background. A few years back our department used to have a light blue shirt and dark blue pants. They went to a darker shirt because you could be working 15 minutes and the next thing you know, your light blue shirt is filthy dirty. On a dark blue shirt, it doesn't show up as much.

Q: Do you like being called "the fuzz"?
A: It doesn't matter to me. A lot of people don't like being called a cop. Why, I don't know. "Cop" used to stand for "Constable On Patrol" and now it's an acronym for "Community Oriented Police" officer.

Q: Is there anything good about working at night, when everyone else is sleeping?

A: Your police work happens at night. During the day there are a lot more people around. When you work at night, there's less traffic and less people, so when you're searching for a suspect, you can easily pick him out.

Late Game

The first major league night baseball game was played at Ebbets Field in Brooklyn, New York, on June 15, 1938. The Cincinnati Reds beat the Brooklyn Dodgers, 6-0, behind Johnny Vander Meer's no-hitter.

91

CHAT WITH A NIGHT CLERK

Store 24 employee Damon Gaudette took a short break to give us the skinny on working the midnight-to-7 A.M. shift at an all-night convenience store.

Q: Why do you keep tuna fish behind the counter?

A: People steal it.

Q: What's the best part of working at night?

A: At night it's cleaner and quiet. I'll sometimes come outside and look at the sky. Also, we make $7.25 an hour if we work days, $8.25 if we work at night. In fact, I was just offered the assistant manager position for the day and I said no for the fifth time in a row because it would be a deduction in pay.

Q: What's the worst thing about working at night?

A: Everyone else is on a day schedule so I can never go shopping after work because the stores aren't open yet. All my friends, including my girlfriend, are asleep when I get home. I don't have a social life.

Q: Have you met any famous people on the job?
A: Steven Wright, the comedian.

Q: What are the best-selling items after midnight?
A: Cigarettes and condoms.

Q: How about beef jerky?
A: Beef jerky is big in the morning.

Q: Have you always been a night person?
A: In high school, I was usually up until three or four in the morning and I'd take a nap after school. I had a lot of brothers and sisters and it was quieter at night.

Q: What's the busiest time of night?
A: Between midnight and three o'clock. The slowest time is between four and six in the morning.

Q: Are you ever tempted to roller-skate in the aisles?
A: No. But when nobody's in the store I like to talk to the products, and I like to yell and sing.

CALLING DR. MIDNIGHT

Dr. Irvin Heifitz

runs the Emergency Room at Newton-Wellesley Hospital in Massachusetts. He used to work the ER at the University of Massachusetts Medical Center.

Q: How many people come into the ER at night?

A: On an average night shift, we might see a dozen patients. But when I worked at the trauma center at UMass, there would be nights when there were car accidents, and people with severe illnesses, and gunshot wounds, and heart attacks and we had to treat them all. Then again, there'd be some nights when we'd sit around playing cards.

Q: Do people really come to the ER to get their ears cleaned?

A: Not exactly. A patient might have a pain in his ear or may have lost hearing in one ear. Maybe we can see very clearly that he needs to have his ears cleaned. Even though the bottom line might be wax in the ears, the symptoms that bring it to your attention might potentially point to something worse. There could be a perforated ear drum, there could be an infection in the ear. There are even certain kinds of tumors that cause pain in that region.

Q: How do you keep patients from falling out of bed?

A: There are railings on the stretchers, and on the gurneys. It's actually a hospital regulation that whenever there isn't a nurse or doctor in the room with a patient, the railings must be up and in a locked position.

Q: Do you ever nap on the job?

A: On the rare occasion, when there is nobody in the department, you might lie down. There's a small room with a cot in the back of the department.

Q: Have you ever had a power blackout at the hospital?

A: Yes, but fortunately all hospitals are required to have an emergency back-up generator system. We once had a squirrel gnaw through a power line, but we had the generator ready.

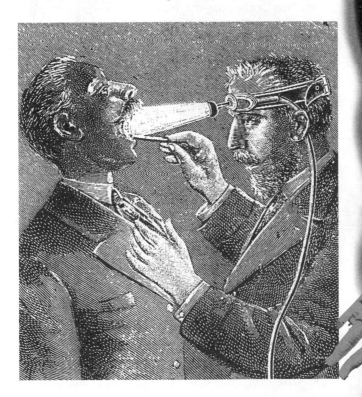

SOME Really Weird (BUT REAL) MUSEUMS

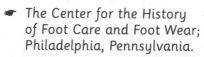

- The Center for the History of Foot Care and Foot Wear; Philadelphia, Pennsylvania.
- The US National Tick Collection (contains about one million dead ticks in 120,000 vials of alcohol); Statesboro, Georgia.

- The Frog Fantasies Museum; Eureka Springs, Arkansas.
- The Nut Museum (admission is a slight fee and a nut); Old Lyme, Connecticut.
- The American Sanitary Plumbing Museum; Worcester, Massachusetts.
- The Crayola Hall of Fame; Easton, Pennsylvania.
- The Teddy Bear Museum; Naples, Florida.
- The Cookie Jar Museum; Lemont, Illinois.
- The Museum of Questionable Medical Devices; Minneapolis, Minnesota.
- The Hair Museum; Independence, Missouri.

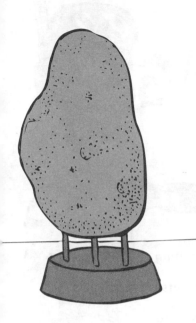

☞ The Lunch Box Museum; Columbus, Georgia.

☞ Marvin Johnson's Gourd Museum (open during daylight; gourds from around the world); Fuguay-Varina, North Carolina.

☞ The Tooth Fairy Museum; Deerfield, Illinois.

☞ McDonald's Museum #1 Store (the restaurant opened in 1955); Des Plaines, Illinois.

☞ The Barbie Hall of Fame; Palo Alto, California.

☞ The Church of One Tree Museum (a church made out of a single redwood tree. The 275-foot-tall tree yielded 78,000 boards of lumber); Santa Rosa, California.

☞ The Potato Museum; Albuquerque, New Mexico.

☞ The Combat Cockroach Hall of Fame; Plano, Texas.

The MELTING Pot

The United States has long been called a melting pot because of our tradition of welcoming immigrants into our country. Here are a few people who came to the United States from other places.

- Madeleine Albright, U.S. Secretary of State, Czechoslovakia
- Mario Andretti, race-car driver, Italy
- Ann-Margaret, actress/singer, Sweden
- Clive Barnes, theater critic, *New York Post*, England
- Saul Bellow, author, Canada
- David Byrne, musician, Talking Heads, Scotland
- Jose Canseco, baseball star, Cuba

- Liz Claiborne, fashion designer, Belgium
- Gloria Estefan, singer, Cuba
- Patrick Ewing, basketball star, Jamaica
- Max Frankel, executive editor, *The New York Times*, Germany
- Terry George, screenwriter, "In the Name of the Father," Ireland
- Peter Jennings, network anchor, Canada
- Ted Koppel, "Nightline" anchor, England
- Angela Lansbury, actress, England
- Yo-Yo Ma, cellist, France
- Peter Max, artist, Germany
- Zubin Mehta, conductor, India
- Martina Navratilova, tennis star, Czechoslovakia
- Mike Nichols, director of "The Graduate," "The Birdcage," Germany
- Hakeem Olajuwon, basketball star, Nigeria
- Frank Oz, puppeteer and film director, England
- I.M. Pei, architect, China
- Itzhak Perlman, classical musician, Israel
- Sidney Poitier, actor, Bahamas
- Anthony Quinn, actor, Mexico
- Carlos Santana, rock musician, Mexico
- General John Shalikashvili, Chairman, Joint Chiefs of Staff, Poland
- Gene Simmons, rock musician, Kiss, Israel
- Elizabeth Taylor, actress, England
- Alex Trotman, CEO, Ford Motor Company, Scotland
- Eddie Van Halen, rock musician, Van Halen, the Netherlands
- Elie Wiesel, author, Romania
- Billy Wilder, director of "Some Like It Hot," Austria
- Neil Young, musician, Canada

WE LOVE THE DRIVE-IN

"Every time I have a date, there's only one place to go, that's to the drive-in. It's such a groovy place to talk and maybe watch a show, down at the drive-in."

— "Drive-In," The Beach Boys, 1964

The Beach Boys are singing this for a good reason. Their home state, California, is second only to Texas in drive-in movie theaters. In 1964, when the song was recorded, California operated 202 drive-ins. If the Beach Boys had been from Nevada, where only 9 drive-ins operated, they might have written a song called "Slot Machine."

Close your eyes. Picture a hot summer night. You want to see a movie but the lines are long at the theater and you're sick of scampering over the sticky floor for a cramped seat. Wouldn't it be nice to drive right up to the screen and watch the flick without getting out of your car?

That's exactly what Richard Milton Hollingshead Jr. thought when he opened the first drive-in theater in Camden, New Jersey on June 6, 1933. For $1 a car, you lined up in one of the rows in front of the 30-foot-high screen and square speaker that blasted out the sound.

Drive-ins began to grow.

- By 1938, there were 50 in the country.
- By 1946, there were 100.
- By 1949, there were 1,000.

Drive-ins were ideal for families. They offered a cheap night out without the hassle of finding a seat. Drive-ins catered to all ages.

- In San Antonio, Texas, you could spend the minutes before show time dancing on a stage constructed near the screen.

- In Wisconsin, a strong man and an acrobat would perform until it was dark enough to show the feature.

- In South Carolina, the theater ran a shopping service. That's right. You handed off a grocery list at the front and got your food delivered during the movie.

- In Long Island, workers did your laundry while you watched. How popular were drive-ins? In the late '40s, a group of angry baby sitters picketed an outdoor theater near Seattle, Washington. They were losing valuable business from former customers who had started taking their children to the drive-in. One protester held up a sign that read: "While you drive in movie theaters, baby sitters starve." The baby sitters drove a hard bargain. They stopped protesting only when the theater owner gave them hot dogs and free movie tickets.

Forty years ago, there were more than 4,000 drive-ins. Today, there are less than 900. The invention of cable TV and VCRs have had a lot to do with the decline. Also, today's cars are much smaller than the gas-guzzlers popular during the glory days of the drive-in. But the biggest factor has been the megaplex. A movie owner can cram six theaters into the space of one outdoor theater. So if you get a chance to spend a night at the drive-in, take it. The summer only lasts so long.

A Drive-In QUIZ

In 1958, at the peak of drive-ins...

...the president was
a. Abraham Lincoln
b. Susan B. Anthony
c. Ernest Hemingway
d. Dwight Eisenhower

...Chuck Berry
a. invented the hula hoop
b. recorded a song called "Johnny B. Goode"
c. bought his favorite golf club
d. opened up Alaska's first juice bar

...The New York Yankees won
a. the lottery
b. a free shopping spree at the local 7-Eleven
c. The World Series
d. A slam dunk contest over Shaq

. . . _____ was not a popular movie.

a. "Cat on a Hot Tin Roof"
b. "Gigi"
c. "Touch of Evil"
d. "Indiana Jones and the Edsel of Doom"

Answers:
1. d; 2. b; 3. c; 4. d.

Other Names for Drive-ins

ozoners ▼ ramp-houses ▼ underskyers ▼
mudholes ▼ fresh-air exhibitors
▼ auto havens ▼ rampitoriums ▼ under-
the-stars emporiums ▼ autodeons
▼ autotoriums ▼ passion pits

Drive-In Timeline
See How the Number of Drive-Ins Rose . . . and Fell

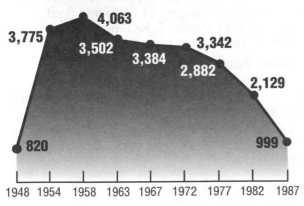

3,775
4,063
3,502
3,384
3,342
2,882
2,129
820
999

1948 1954 1958 1963 1967 1972 1977 1982 1987

True Stories

(SUPPOSEDLY)

The Homecoming

Charles Coughlan was born in the Canadian province of Prince Edward Island. He moved to Galveston, Texas, to perform in an actors' troupe and died there suddenly in 1899.

One year later, a massive flood destroyed the town. Not only were 8,000 Galvestonians killed, but the ocean waves destroyed the cemeteries.

Coughlan's lead coffin floated into the Gulf Stream, past the Florida Keys, and headed north, up the Atlantic. In 1908, eight years later, a group of fisherman spotted the box off the coast of Prince Edward Island. Coughlan's body had floated back to within a mile of the Church in which he had been christened.

Electric Personality

Roy Cleveland Sullivan was known as the "Human Lightning Rod." He got struck the first time in 1942, in his big toe. Over the next 36 years, he would be hit on his left shoulder, eyebrows, hair, stomach, and chest. He lived through it all.

Freakiest Story in This Whole Book

The temperature in Milwaukee, Wisconsin dropped to 60° below zero on January 19, 1985. That's when two-year-old Michael Troche wandered outside in just his pajamas. His parents, who were asleep, didn't find him for several hours. By that time, Michael had been frozen as stiff as a board. He was no longer breathing and his body temperature had fallen to 16 degrees. Doctors could hear his body crack as they moved him.

At Milwaukee Children's Hospital, Michael was hooked up to a machine to warm his blood. Doctors also made little cuts in his body like you might to a hot dog about to be grilled. His blood was so frozen and full of water, they worried he might burst when he began to melt! After three days between life and death, Michael recovered, with only minor injuries. Why? The doctors said his size saved him. His tiny brain needed much less oxygen than an adult's would have to operate. If he had been older, Michael would have been a goner.

Haunted Ship

The S.S. Watertown oil tanker left New York City for the Panama Canal in the winter of 1924. On the way, two crewmen, James Courtney and Michael Meehan, died accidentally when they were overcome by fumes while cleaning the gas tank.

The next day, the ship's captain noticed a spooky sight following the ship: the glowing faces of Courtney and Meehan in the water. The captain snapped several photos of the phantoms, one of which showed the faces clearly. The S.S. Watertown's owners put a large copy of one photo in the lobby of their main office in New York City.

Crazy Vampires

Dracula's real name was Prince Vlad IV, or Vlad the Impaler. He ruled Romania in the 15th century and was so cruel he would drink or bathe in the blood of those he was torturing. When he died in 1477, rumor had it that Vlad would rise from the dead in search of more blood.

There was also a female vampire. Elizabeth Bathory was born in 1560 and married a count when she was only 15. But later, with her beauty fading, she ordered a young maid murdered. Bathory then took a bath in the young maid's blood, convinced it could rejuvenate her. Did it? Of course not. Bathory was judged insane and jailed until her death, in 1614.

Raining Cats and . . . Frogs

What do you do when it's raining frogs? Nothing if you're in Nauplia, Greece. In May of 1981, the citizens of the town woke to find thousands of the green creatures falling from the sky. Scientists told them not to worry: a whirlwind from North Africa had sucked the frogs into the air and brought them across the Mediterranean.

TAKE THE Ice Cream QUIZ

1. During the Civil War, Confederate soldiers were rewarded with ice cream sodas for a victory on the battlefield.
True   **False**

2. Americans eat enough ice cream each year to fill the Grand Canyon.
True   **False**

3. Thomas Edison invented ice cream.
True   **False**

4. The largest ice cream sundae was served at the coronation of Henry V of England.
True   **False**

1. False. The ice cream soda wasn't invented until nine years after the Civil War, in 1874. Robert Green, a vendor in Philadelphia, was making egg creams (a drink made with sweet cream, syrup and carbonated water) and ran out of cream. He replaced it with vanilla ice cream. Green's new drink was an immediate hit. When he died, "Originator of the Ice Cream Soda" was chiseled onto his gravestone.

2. True. Americans eat one billion gallons of ice cream a year. That's an average of 175 cones per person every year. That's more than any other country in the world.

3. False. Sometime in the 16th century, a frozen milk dessert began to be served to elite Italians. A slightly modified ice cream didn't get sold to regular folks until 1670, at a cafe in Paris. The cool treat made it to America about 30 years later and our first President, George Washington, considered it his favorite dessert.

4. False. The largest ice cream sundae was built in 1975 in McClean, Virginia. It weighed 3,956 pounds and called for 777 gallons of ice cream, a case of chocolate sprinkles, six gallons of chocolate sauce and a gallon of whipped cream. The largest banana split, created in St. Paul, Minnesota, called for 10,000 bananas and 33,000 scoops of ice cream. The world's largest popsicle wasn't quite so impressive. It weighed only 2,800 pounds.

SPOOKY

MATCH

Can you match the spooky story with the state in which it was reported? Select your answer from the list and write it in the box with each story.

a. New Jersey   **b.** Florida
c. Colorado   **d.** Ohio
e. Missouri   **f.** Tennessee
g. Indiana   **h.** California
i. Georgia   **j.** Michigan

1. In July 1966, two teenaged girls told police they'd seen a hairy, seven-foot-tall "bush beast" covered in moss and slime. More than 200 people joined forces for a massive monster hunt, but they never did find him.

2. A man called Rush Limbaugh's radio show on October 24, 1990 to report he'd seen a hairy, giant beast near Pike's Peak.

3. Ralph "Bud" Chambers heard a loud cough as he walked through the woods. He turned and spotted a seven-foot-tall hairy creature a few feet away. "The thing had a rancid, putrid odor like stale urine," said Chambers. He added that the monster was at least four feet wide.

Answers: 1. h; 2. c; 3. b; 4. i; 5. g; 6. j; 7. e; 8. a; 9. d; 10. f.

108

4. A hairy, three-foot-tall man was seen running out of the woods. Strands of white, curly hair were spotted at the scene and a local crime lab reported they were human. A zoologist suggested it could have been a kangaroo.

5. Several teen-agers hanging out in a grave-yard saw a red-eyed, seven-foot-tall creature. It stood up like a human, but ran on four legs. Footprints showed four long toes.

6. Two men reported that an ape-like crea-ture picked them up briefly and then, after dropping them, ran away. They said the monster had green eyes "as big as light bulbs" and "smelled like something rotten."

7. In the late '40s, a creature was reported to be ripping cows and horses apart and leav-ing their carcasses to rot. Someone killed the animal and said it looked like a gorilla.

8. At sundown, four men were parked near the Morristown Historical Park when they saw a seven-foot-tall creature wandering toward them. They said it had no face, was covered with long hair, and had scaly skin. The men drove to the park entrance to warn others not to enter and reported the sighting at the local police station.

9. Several people report that a "monster man" has been living in a cemetery tunnel for 25 years. One woman described the creature as big and hairy and weighing 400 pounds.

10. A man captured in the woods was put on exhibition because his eyes were twice the size of normal eyes and his body was covered with fish scales. They called him the "Wild Man of the Woods."

Excuse Me?
In some Southern towns, they refer to the hairy, tall creature, usually known as "bigfoot," as "booger."

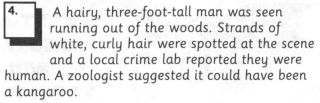

Bed Biz

Y ou toss in it, you turn on it, you dream in it, and at some point you've fallen out of it. Your bed.

The earliest ones had no mattresses, box springs, or headboards. They were the ground. After a hard day of doing things like discovering fire, cavefolks spent their nights on dirty slabs of earth.

It didn't get much better for thousands of years. The Egyptians built beds using palm leaves and wicker. In Ancient China, the pillows were made of wood, or stone (!). During the Middle Ages, most peasants slept in the barn, on the dirt floor, with the animals.

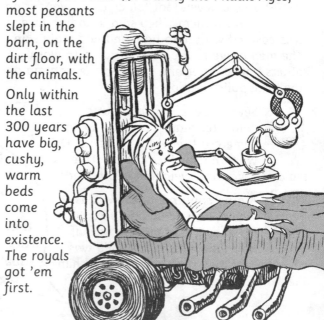

Only within the last 300 years have big, cushy, warm beds come into existence. The royals got 'em first.

Have you ever had to share a bed? If so, we suggest you ask your bed mate — brother, sister, friend, pet — to sign the following contract:

A Bed Contract

I will not:

☞ write all over your face with a crayon while you sleep

☞ hog the covers

☞ steal your pillow and fill it with green slime

☞ suck your thumb

☞ practice how to tango

☞ eat sugar cookies, unless of course I share a few

signature

witness

date

Princess Isabella of Portugal had one built that was 19 feet by 12 and a half feet.

The Great Bed of Ware, which still exists in England, is nine feet tall and 11 feet long. King Louis XIV of France had 413 beds. His favorite had crimson curtains covered in real gold.

In the 18th Century, metal began to replace wood as a bed-building material. There were less fleas that way. The next 100 years brought about the creation of the spiral mattress and box springs.

Earlier this century, Howard Hughes, the reclusive billionaire, had a bed made for him that used 30 electric motors to move him in whatever way he pleased. The bed also supplied hot and cold running water. Imagine, a cup of hot chocolate without crawling out from under your covers.

TIME FOR A BED CHECK

BECAUSE

you will spend more than 200,000 hours in bed during your lifetime, it's important to make sure to get the proper equipment for sleeping.

1. Mattress

The average mattress lasts 10 years. That means you better make a good choice when you're deciding what kind to buy.

Here are the different kinds:

Name of bed	Width	Length
Twin	38 inches	75 inches
Double or full	53–54 inches	75 inches
Queen	60 inches	80 inches
National/Eastern King	76 inches	80 inches
California King	72 inches	84 inches

The more coils in your mattress, the better. A good, king-size model should have between 450 and 600 coils.

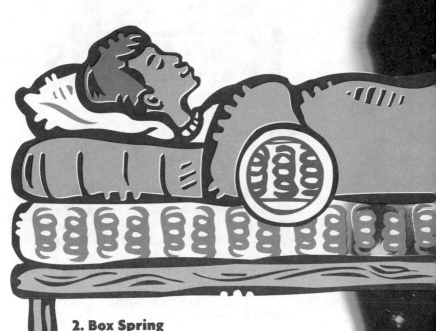

2. Box Spring

It might seem unnecessary because it sits under your mattress, but a box spring is essential to your sleeping comfort. Box springs are your bed's foundation and support, absorbing the nightly wear and tear that occurs when we move around. The average sleeper shifts in bed between 40 and 60 times a night.

3. Waterbed

Waterbeds used to be huge bags full of water, basically. Sloshy and uncomfortable. These days, waterbeds are highly sensitive sleeping devices with several different parts. The water mattress is made of vinyl and has rounded corners. The liner fits between you and the mattress. Even if there's a leak in your mattress, the liner should keep you dry. The frame is like any other frame, except it must support the weight of a waterbed.

If worse comes to worst and you can't find a good bed, you might want to make like a hedgehog and find a nice pile of leaves to hibernate under.

Bed Records

Most expensive bed: $75,000. A 1930 black lacquer king-size bed made by Jean Durand and auctioned at Christie's in New York City.

Fastest bed-making speed: 19 seconds. Sisters Jill Bradbury and Chris Humpish of London made the bed with a blanket, two sheets, an undersheet, pillow, and a bedspread.

Longest endurance on a bed of nails: 300 hours. Ken Owen, 48, of the U.K. lay on a bed of nails from May 3rd to May 14th in 1986. That included 132 hours, 30 minutes without a break.

Furthest bed pushing: 3,233 miles. Nine workers at Bruntsfield Bedding Centre in Edinburgh, Scotland, pushed a bed from June 21 to July 26, 1979.

Smelly, Buggy Bed Mattresses in medieval England were a nightmare. Rats and mice nested in them, bringing smelly and extremely dead prey along for a nightcap. Things got better, but not by much, in the 18th century when mattresses stuffed with leaves, pine needles, and reeds became moldy and bug-ridden.

At the same time, in France, people tried to make sleeping more comfortable, inventing the first air mattresses and mattresses stuffed with human hair.

10 THINGS
ACTUALLY SAID BY OUR
41 ST PRESIDENT, GEORGE BUSH:

"I'm not the most articulate emotionalist."

"I've told you I don't live and die by the polls. Thus I will refrain from pointing out that we're not doing too bad in those polls."

"It has been said by some cynic, maybe it was a former president, 'If you want a friend in Washington, get a dog.' We took them literally — that advice — as you know. But I didn't need that, because I have Barbara Bush."

"I put confidence in the American people, in their ability to sort through what is fair and what is unfair, what is ugly and what is unugly."

"When I need a little free advice about Saddam Hussein, I turn to country music."

"It's no exaggeration to say the undecideds could go one way or another."

"Please just don't look at part of the glass, the part that is only less than half full."

"Those are two hypo-rhetorical questions."

"I'm not going to hypothecate that it may — anything goes too fast."

"Fluency in English is something that I'm often not accused of."

·T·H·E· Secret Truth About PAJAMAS

This is probably the golden age of bed clothing. Think about it. The choices are almost endless: pajamas, underwear, nightshirts, nightgowns, sweat pants, or . . . nothing at all.

Yep, that's right — nude. Twenty-six percent of men sleep in the buff, as opposed to six percent of women.

Which brings us to the next point. For some reason, American women have always gotten a raw deal in night clothing. Less freedom, fewer choices.

Back in the 1870s, men wore comfortable nightshirts and funny-looking nightcaps called "jellybags." Women, on the other hand, were expected to sleep in linen dresses that touched the floor and had ruffles up to the neck. Not exactly sweats and a T-shirt. In the next decade, two-piece pajamas were introduced — FOR MEN ONLY. Women were stuck with nightdresses until the early part of the 20th century. Even then, the women who chose pajamas were younger and less conservative. That's right, pajama-wearers were rebels.

Women didn't get truly comfortable night clothing until the 1940s. The 1947 Sears catalog lists a two-piece pajama suit with a tie-top bra and shorts for $3.98. The 1950 catalog shows a wool flannel bathrobe for $8.96 and nylon lingerie for just $4.49.

The tradition of inequality might be said to continue in a subtle fashion even today, with men being more comfortable with nude napping. So sleep naked. (Only if you want to, of course.) Because there will be a time when what you sleep in is not just given to you. And when that time comes, you've got to be ready. Who knows? Maybe you'll want a linen dress.

"One morning I shot an elephant in my pajamas. How he got in my pajamas I'll never know."
—Groucho Marx

A First

The first nightdress was reportedly worn by Isidore, a Spanish scholar and saint, in the 1600s.

Boxers in Bed

Men didn't start wearing boxer shorts to bed until the early part of the 20th century, when central heating became more popular.

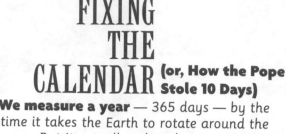

FIXING THE CALENDAR (or, How the Pope Stole 10 Days)

We measure a year — 365 days — by the time it takes the Earth to rotate around the sun. But it actually takes closer to 365.25 days for the Earth to travel its orbit. At that rate, we gain a day every four years.

The Romans took the first step toward fixing the calendar 2,000 years ago by tacking on an extra day every four years and calling it a leap year. Problem solved. Right? **Wrong.**

It turns out the Earth's rotation takes almost 365.25, but not exactly. This means nothing in the short run — the discrepancy amounts to only .75 of an extra day over 100 years. But over centuries, the extra time adds up.

Pope Gregory had the solution. In 1582, the Pope determined that certain leap years should be eliminated: those that fall on a year that ends in 00 and whose first two digits are not divisible by four. (1700 and 1900, for example, but not 2000.)

To fix the problem, the Pope had to do something about the 10 "extra" days that had built up since the Romans created leap years. So he declared that October 5 to October 14 simply wouldn't exist that year. It wasn't an easy sell — people were losing 10 days of their lives — but it stuck because he was the Pope. Only two countries held out: England until 1751 and Russia until 1918.

Light Night

Anchorage, Alaska is the southernmost spot where you can see the sun circle the sky on Summer Solstice — the longest day of the year. Minor league baseball teams often start their games after 10 p.m. because it never gets totally dark.

CAN YOU SOLVE These Broken Telescope Mysteries?

Problem: Researchers at Ohio State University were searching for signs of life in space when their computer broke down because the air supply to the machine's disk drive has been cut off. Why?

Answer: A mouse had built a nest inside the computer. The nest clogged up the disk drive.

Problem: A telescope at the Royal Greenwich Observatory in Australia stopped working because its cross-hairs, the fine strands of wire that help the viewer focus on an object, were broken. Replacing them isn't easy: a strand of human hair is four times the size of a cross-hair. How did the cross-hairs get broken?

Answer: A fly entered the telescope and died. The dead fly's body crushed the cross-hairs.

Problem: Two astronomers studying stars at the Haute Provence Observatory in France saw bright lights in their telescope's viewer and decided they were evidence of the chemical potassium burning and flaring as it entered the atmosphere. That is almost unheard of when dealing with the particular stars they were studying, so when they published a paper on the finding, the scientific world was intrigued. But in the next few years, nobody was able to find those same kind of flares. What happened?

Answer: While working, one of the astronomers struck a match to light a cigarette. A piece of the match lodged in the telescope. Matches, incidentally, contain potassium. That's where the spark came from.

REMEMBER THESE THINGS

(And You'll Know a Lot of Weird Stuff)

The Six Continents
Africa
Antartica
Australia
Eurasia
North America
South America

The Five Marx Brothers
Chico
Groucho
Harpo
Zeppo
Gummo

The Five Families
(of organized crime in New York City):
Bonanno
Colombo
Gambino
Genovese
Lucchese

The Six Senses
sight
hearing
smell
taste
touch
clairvoyance

The Seven Dwarfs
Dopey
Doc
Grumpy
Happy
Sleepy
Bashful
Sneezy

Four Corners

(Near Teec Nos Pas, a town in Arizona, the boundaries of these four states meet)
Arizona
Utah
Colorado
New Mexico

The Three Little Pigs

Fifer Pig, who built his house out of straw
Fiddler Pig, who used wood
Practical Pig, who used brick

Santa's Eight Reindeer

Blitzen
Comet
Cupid
Dancer
Dasher
Donder
Prancer
Vixen

Three Branches of Government

Legislative
Executive
Judicial

The Thirteen Original Colonies

Connecticut
Delaware
Georgia
Maine
Maryland
Massachusetts
New Hampshire
New York
North Carolina
Pennsylvania
Rhode Island
South Carolina
Virginia

Three Men In a Tub

The butcher
The baker
The candlestick maker

The Seven Deadly Sins

Pride
Lust
Gluttony
Anger
Envy
Sloth
Covetousness

The Six Categories of Nobel Prizes

Peace
Chemistry
Physics
Physiology of Medicine
Literature
Economics

121

WHAT'S YOUR SIGN DUDE?

So you have trouble telling the difference between astronomy and astrology? Not surprising. Both start with an A and end with a Y. In fact, there are only two letters that separate the two words. But here's why it's important you understand why astronomy and astrology aren't even as close as second cousins.

If astronomy is about charting the physical location of everything in space, astrology is about trying to figure out how these planets and stars influence our lives. For example, an astronomer will tell you where to find Venus on a chart of the solar system. An astrologer will tell you how Venus makes girls and boys born between April 20 and May 20 more determined than girls and boys born between September 23 and October 22.

Some people have a word for that kind of analysis: Hooey!

And yes, astrology is often dismissed as nothing but superstition. But what the doubters can't deny is the influence of astrology. Just check out the daily horoscope in your morning paper. Know who wrote that horoscope? An astrologer, that's who.

A horoscope is a map showing the positions of the planets at the time of a birth. There are 12 signs — just as there are 12 months — but the signs don't correspond to our calendar year. In fact, the first day of an astrological year is March 21.

So next time it's March 21, make sure to wish everyone a "Happy New Year."

Now comes the cool part: finding your sign.

ARIES **March 21–April 19** Arians are full of energy, enthusiasm, and competitive spirit. This near obsession with being #1 does cause them to become impatient quickly. **Other Arians:** Claire Danes, Leonard Nimoy, Cy Young, Diana Ross, Mariah Carey.

TAURUS **April 20–May 20** Taureans like good clothing, consider physical appearance important, and value material possessions. Taureans can be very loyal to friends, but they are also unnecessarily jealous at times. **Other Taureans:** Stevie Wonder, William Shakespeare, Ella Fitzgerald, Dennis Rodman, Uma Thurman, Barbara Streisand.

GEMINI **May 21–June 21** Geminis are good talkers. They like to be considered intellectuals and sometimes rebel against the status quo. When they get older, they usually learn to cooperate. **Other Geminis:** Tim Allen, Nicole Kidman, Bob Dylan, Miles Davis, Helen Hunt.

CANCER **June 22–July 22** Cancers are sensitive and interested in getting married and building a family. They are neat and dislike anything that is dirty. **Other Cancers:** Princess Di, Bill Cosby, Ringo Starr.

LEO **July 23–August 22** Leos are confident, outspoken, aggressive, and fiercely protective of their children. They are always looking for approval from others. **Other Leos:** Whitney Houston, Annie Oakley, Madonna, Kenny Rogers, Herman Melville.

VIRGO **August 23–September 22** Virgos are known for their need for order and structure. Sometimes they get too focused on work, which can lead to boring conversations. Many Virgos never marry, and tend to spend money freely. **Other Virgos:** Cal Ripkin Jr., Jonathan Taylor Thomas, Charlie Parker, Sean Connery, Confucius.

LIBRA September 23–October 22 Libras have bad tempers and tend to be aaaressive in an argument. But they're also go companions, and like to run activities involving groups. **Other Libras:** Sting, Yo-Yo Ma, Christopher Reeve, John Lithgow, Will Smith.

SCORPIO October 23–November 21 Scorpios sometimes get so involved in a task that they will overwork and overstress. Physically, they are usually muscular and tall. **Other Scorpios:** Roseanne, Pablo Picasso, Pele, Winona Ryder, Dan Rather, Whoopi Goldberg.

SAGITTARIUS November 22–December 21 Sagittarians are honest and generous, but sometimes quick to jump to conclusions. They are free thinkers and outgoing. **Other Sagittarians:** Jane Fonda, Tina Turner, Joe Dimaggio, Charles "Peanuts" Schultz.

CAPRICORN December 22–January 19  Capricorns like to be the boss, at work and at home. They thirst for money, fearing without it they'll have to depend on someone else. They can sometimes get lonely. **Other Capricorns:** Jim Carrey, Martin Luther King Jr., Mary Tyler Moore, Elvis Presley.

AQUARIUS January 20–February 18 Aquarians value their friends. They can be stubborn and argumentative, but they always go back to the group because they enjoy teamwork. **Other Acquarians:** Oprah Winfrey, Sheryl Crow, Jackie Robinson, John Travolta.

PISCES February 19–March 20 Pisceans don't have strong willpower and they also have trouble making up their minds. They are funny, charming, and hate to argue. But sometimes they can forget to take care of simple tasks. **Other Pisceans:** Drew Barrymore, Shaquille O'Neal, Elizabeth Taylor, Liza Minnelli.

Horseradish for Toothaches!

Folk Remedies

The most famous of them all is chicken soup. If you get a cold, the age-old theory goes, there's nothing better than a piping hot bowl of grandma's homemade chicken soup. Sounds natural, right? But why?

Because like most folk remedies, the soup treatment has been passed down over generations. Other home-grown prescriptions cover everything from cold feet to hot fevers. Folk remedies are based on tradition, not medical science, which is why you should never consider them a replacement for a trip to the hospital. Why try them? As the saying goes, "It couldn't hurt."

The big downside to folk remedies, which you'll realize as soon as you start reading about them on the following pages, is that they can be extremely gross. To improve your memory, for example, folk medics recommend a glass of milk and carrot juice mixed together.

Some of us would rather be forgetful.

A note of caution: even the most dedicated home-remediest says that when you're really sick, you should go see a doctor. Who knows . . . maybe a doctor might suggest a better way to get rid of a migraine than placing cabbage leaves on your forehead.

SICKNESS & REMEDIES

Cold, flu 1. Chicken soup is a proven aid in times of sickness. This was concluded in 1978 through an informal study at the Mount Sinai Medical Center in Miami. 2. Garlic is often referred to as the Russian penicillin. One treatment plan suggests you keep a peeled clove of garlic between your cheek and teeth for four hours (don't chew on it). Another folk remediest suggests mixing six crushed cloves of garlic with half a cup of lard, and spreading the mess on the bottoms of your feet. If your feet didn't smell before, they will after.

Bloody noses Stick your hands in warm water.

Depression Throw some watercress, spinach, and carrots into a blender and drink the muck down. (This is going to cheer you up?) Also, eat lots of bananas and oregano, though not necessarily together.

Black eye Put a cold, raw steak on the eye.

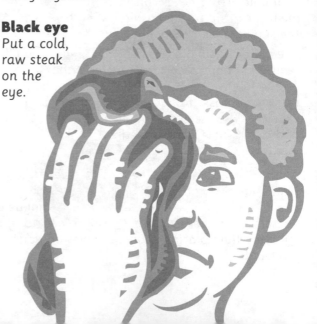

Night vision Eat, or drink the juice of, three carrots a day. Consume blueberries and watercress, too.

Sore and tired feet During the day, when you can't get to a nice, warm bath, there's a simple solution for sore feet: cayenne pepper. Yep, sprinkle it into your socks or directly onto the bottoms of your feet. One warning: don't let your socks get into the soup. That cayenne pepper stuff is hot.

Headaches 1. Dip a handkerchief in vinegar and place it around your forehead until the headache is gone. 2. Stand in freezing water up to your ankles. As soon as your feet begin to adjust to the temperature, leave the tub for your bed.` 3. Take a teaspoon of honey mixed with 1/2 teaspoon of garlic juice.

Hiccups 1. Put an ice cube on your throat and count to 150. 2. Inhale a small amount of pepper. Sneeze a couple of times. 3. Take seven sips of water without breathing.

Bed wetting Chew on cinnamon bark for a day.

Misery brought on by sorrow that this book is over 1. Read this book again. 2. Read the books mentioned on the next page.